Social Movements, Violence and Change

William A. Anderson
and Russell R. Dynes

# Social Movements
# Violence and Change

## The May Movement in Curaçao

Ohio State University Press: Columbus

Photographs used as the Frontispiece and on the endsheets
are reproduced by permission of *Amigoe di Curaçao*.

Copyright © 1975 by the Ohio State University Press
All rights reserved
Manufactured in the United States of America

Library of Congress Cataloging in Publication Data
Anderson, William Averette, 1937-

Social movements, violence, and change.

Includes bibliographical references and index.
1. Curaçao—Social conditions. 2. Labor and laboring classes—Curaçao. 3. Violence
—Curaçao. I. Dynes, Russell Rowe, 1923- II. Title.
HN247.A53          301.24'2'0972986          75-6769
ISBN 0-8142-0240-3

*to Candice, Norma and Sue*

# Contents

LIST OF TABLES

LIST OF ILLUSTRATIONS

# Preface

When we first casually read a brief account of the May, 1969, violence in Curaçao in a local newspaper, little did we know at the time that we would become involved in a study of events taking place there over a two-year period, and would make three field trips to the small island. We both had an interest in the sociology of the human response to crisis, and had been involved in studies on natural disasters and civil disturbances. This interest led us to undertake the present study, which we found to be a most rewarding intellectual experience.

The focus of this study is upon the May Movement, the violence that initially attracted our attention being only one of its many phases. We have devoted most of our attention to those sociological aspects of the May Movement which we hope will contribute most to furthering the understanding of social movements in general: the conditions that gave rise to the movement; its career; and its consequences for Curaçao and possible implications for the future. The notion of social change has been used to tie these three aspects of the study together. Drawing on the literature in the field, we have attempted to indicate some of the general implications of the study by comparing the May Movement with other social movements.

Many people assisted us in this effort. There were those in

Curaçao, too numerous to mention individually, who gave willingly of their time and knowledge. Researchers from another society could not have asked for better cooperation and hospitality than we received during our field work in Curaçao. We especially appreciate the help of Stanley Brown, A. J. Kusters, and Rolof van Hövel. We also owe a special thanks to fellow sociologist R. A. Römer who read the entire manuscript and offered many valuable suggestions.

The assistance of Norma Anderson, who made valuable comments and typed part of the initial draft of the manuscript, is also appreciated. The study was financed by two grants from Arizona State University's University Grants Committee and a grant from the Ohio State University's Mershon Center. We gratefully acknowledge this support.

Social Movements, Violence and Change

# CHAPTER ONE

# Social Movements and Social Change

This is a study of social protest and change in Curaçao, a small developing island-society in the Caribbean. Located 35 miles north of Venezuela, it is the largest and most populous island of the Netherlands Antilles, a former Dutch colony that also includes Aruba, Bonaire, Saint Maarten, Saba, and Saint Eustatuis. The population of Curaçao is around 141,000, of whom over 65,000 live in Willemstad, the capital of the Antilles.[1]

In studying social change in Curaçao, we have chosen to focus on social movements, especially the May Movement that crystallized in 1969. This movement grew out of a labor dispute and assumed several different forms, the most dramatic being a riot in which there was loss of life, many injuries, and millions of dollars in property damage. One of the local newspapers provides an initial introduction to this event.

> The capital of the Netherlands Antilles, Willemstad, on the last day of May 1969, looks like a city struck by disaster. A tidal wave of violence flooded the city yesterday and it seems many lives were lost and many injured. There has been damage of many millions due to fires and looting on a large scale. Trade has suffered heavy loss and it may be assumed that many people lost their lifework in a few hours time. . . .
> In less than 24 hours, the leaden mask of an unconcerned and

carefree life has been ripped off a large part of Curaçao in the Caribbean Sea. From behind this mask came the ugly face which was lined with suppressed racial sentiments. The view which the world has was one which revealed itself in arson and looting. The myth of the carefreeness of the Antillean people was destroyed abruptly in the burning ruins of buildings.[2]

As the newspaper excerpt suggests, the violent episode surprised many persons because the inhabitants of Curaçao, most of whom are nonwhite, were considered among the most peaceful in the Caribbean and perhaps the most unlikely to engage in radical protest of any sort. It is even doubtful that the few self-proclaimed radicals on the island could anticipate that the inhabitants were prepared to protest in as dramatic fashion as they did, on May 30, such conditions as low wages, high unemployment, and the domination of the economy by local and foreign whites. The central government of the Antilles had attributed the labor tranquility in the society to Antilleans' strong traditional family ties that alledgedly made them immune from radical politics and forms of protest. In fact, this theory was mentioned in a 1965 government publication aimed at prospective foreign investors.

> Antillian families are bound together by unusually strong ties and therefore extremist elements have little chance to interfere in labor relations. There is no communist party. Labor unions and their leaders refrain from excessive demands which might result in more unemployment.[3]

On May 30, 1969, however, this image of the Antilles was dramatically shattered as striking workers were mobilized into the mass movement that we now call the May Movement and that some of the inhabitants refer to as the May Revolution. Thousands of workers, led by black radical and moderate labor leaders and some radical teachers, took to the streets and battled police, harassed whites, and destroyed millions of dollars in property. This violent episode was only one part of the May Movement, but it was certainly an important phase. We will describe it in more detail in order to set the stage for the context in which the May Movement will be examined.

## THE RIOT

The riot in Curaçao had its immediate roots in a labor dispute between the Curaçao Federation of Workers (CFW) and Werkspoor Caribbean (WESCAR), a contractor for the most important business enterprise on the island, the Royal Dutch Shell Company. The CFW was seeking a wage agreement that was equivalent to one that had been negotiated earlier for Shell employees by another union, the Petroleum Workers Federation of Curaçao (PWFC). On May 6, 1969, the CFW led a group of 400 workers on a strike against WESCAR. From this initial action, the labor unrest was to spread to Shell itself and, more important, take on political and racial overtones.

The crucial point during the crisis came on May 30. After calling a sympathy strike against Shell in support of the CFW, members of the PWFC, along with members of several other unions that had also gone on strike against their employers, gathered in the morning at the entrance to the Shell refinery. Labor leaders began making speeches to the crowd, which had grown to an estimated size of between three and four thousand men. A few of these leaders, including one popular figure in particular by the name of Papa Godett who was head of a radical union, began advocating that the strikers' protest take on broader dimensions. Godett called on the strikers to march on Fort Amsterdam, the seat of government located in downtown Willemstad, to overthrow the government, declaring that it was basically responsible for the economic plight of workers, especially black workers. He was quoted as having said, "If we don't succeed without force, then we have to use force. I will lead, but if I get killed, then I want the struggle to continue. . . . But I will lead, and I want you to follow me. The people is the government. The present government is no good and we will replace it."[4]

The crowd began to move toward downtown Willemstad, led by Godett and several other labor leaders, to register its protest with the government. Along the way, cars were overturned and burned and some whites were harassed. Stores were also looted. Youths began participating in the protest march. Before the marchers could reach Fort Amsterdam, they were met by the police, and during the ensuing confrontation Papa Godett was shot. Left leaderless because most of the other union leaders on the march went to the hospital with the wounded Godett and remained there until they saw that he would recover, the bulk of the crowd broke up into smaller groups and quickly spread through the downtown business district breaking windows, looting, and setting fires. Some of the buildings that were set afire by the rioters were several hundred years old and thus burned quickly. Also the compactness of the business district made access difficult for fire-fighting equipment. The fires in the downtown area were not brought under control until the next day, ending the danger of fire spreading to other parts of the city. A curfew was enforced on Friday, May 30, and remained in effect over the weekend. On June 1, Dutch Marines arrived in Curaçao from the Netherlands to provide relief for weary local security forces.

One of the most significant consequences of the disturbance was that the unions, through the threat of calling a general strike, forced the government to resign and call for new elections. In issuing their ultimatum, the unions claimed that the government had "used weapons in order to stop the desires of the workers." This development overshadowed a new agreement negotiated by the CFW with WESCAR during the riot.

There were many persons in Curaçao who attempted to explain what occurred on that "most historic day," May 30, 1969. Among them was a writer, Edward A. de Jongh, who observed the day's events by walking the streets of Willemstad and later wrote a book titled *May 30, 1969: The Most Historic Day*.[5] The author used a fictitious young man named Boy Kalino as the main character in the book. Boy is the youngest son of a fatherless family of three. His sister, Rosita, works at one of the stores owned and operated by a Jewish merchant. His sick mother receives a small amount of relief from public funds, and Boy is unemployed. Through this poor family, de Jongh paints a picture of what he sees as the social causes underlying the rebellion against authority, the wanton destruction, arson, and pilfering on May 30.

Boy Kalino and his family are seen as victims of widespread

unemployment in Curaçao, the lack of adequate social laws (including those governing termination of employment and layoff procedures), and discrimination based on color and race. Boy puts on his one good shirt to go and look for a job. He finds one, but is arbitrarily fired on the very first day as he arrives late through no fault of his own. He is not given the chance to explain what happened. As the story develops, Boy is first a shocked eyewitness to the May 30 events, but then after some liquor he becomes a participant and vents his pent-up aggression by throwing a Molotov cocktail at the store where he was fired. He accepts three very expensive gold watches that were looted from the well-known jewelers Spritzer and Fuhrman and is apprehended and sentenced to jail for seven months.

As de Jongh indicates in his book, the May riot resulted from both immediate and deep-seated problems in the society. Thus the May Movement did not come to an end with the termination of the riot and the government's forced resignation. For example, a group of dissenters formed a new labor party and in the special election held after the May rebellion managed to capture seats in parliament by campaigning on an Antillean nationalist platform. Somewhat later, a second party was formed with an emphasis upon black nationalism.

THE MAY MOVEMENT AS A SYNTHESIS

One of the highest government officials in the Netherlands Antilles astutely observed that the evolution of the May Movement in Curaçao was related to the fact that this Caribbean island, like most societies in the modern world, did not live in isolation from events transpiring in other lands. He pointed to Curaçao's well-developed mass media as a major means whereby information about happenings and circumstances in places like the United States, Europe, South America, and other parts of the Caribbean was channeled onto the island. It could be added too that Antilleans go abroad for many reasons, such as for business and educational purposes, thus having the opportunity to come in contact with new

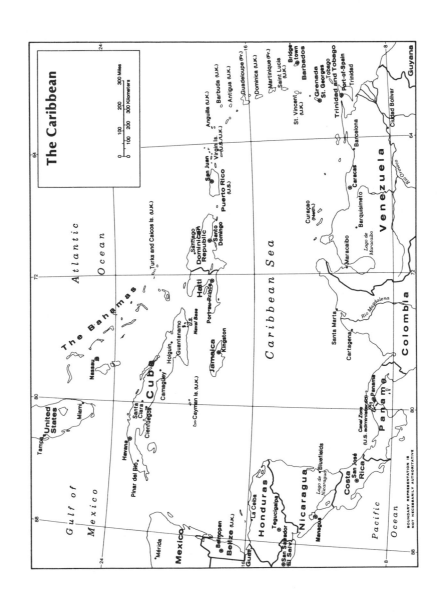

The Caribbean

ideas and perspectives. This has been especially true of students who have gone to universities abroad. Of some importance also is the fact that Antilleans are exposed to many outsiders who visit their country as a result of its location, climate, and oil industry. Its location in the Caribbean makes it a sort of crossroads, as indicated in the following excerpt.

> This capital of the Netherlands Antilles is becoming embroiled again in Caribbean politics. Willemstad, a tranquil center of tourism and Dutch trading has become a relay point for hundreds of political and technical expeditions to Cuba. Because of geography and transportation advantages, Curaçao has long been known as the gateway to the Caribbean from the Latin-American mainland. However, the Government is finding it increasingly embarrassing that the island's role is turning it into a staging area for Cuba-bound Soviet, Czechoslovak and Chinese technicians, Polish ''tourists'' and Latin American ''students.'' The number of ideologically receptive Latin Americans streaming through here toward Cuba is increasing daily. Several hundred arrive monthly.[6]

The climate also attracts many tourists from North America and the Netherlands, and the oil industry has attracted many workers from the Netherlands as well as other Caribbean islands. With Curaçao's openess, then, it is not surprising that the May Movement was a blend of characteristics manifested by movements elsewhere. It articulated themes that could be seen in youth, labor, and ethnic movements found in many parts of the world, including the Caribbean, the United States, and Europe along with many indigenous ideas. These themes were reinterpreted in the light of Curaçao's own sociohistorical experience. This synthesis made the May Movement similar to, yet different from, many other political movements that have emerged around the same period.

The Netherlands Antilles is a developing society, or part of what is now commonly referred to as the Third World. In this part of the world, there are many movements aimed at eradicating color barriers and the political and economic subordination of the masses. In Africa, South America, and the Caribbean, there has been a proliferation of movements attempting to transform colonial and neo-colonial systems. The May Movement is a part of this trend. The recent revolutionary changes Cuba has undergone, of course, have captured the imagination of many developing nations. Unlike what some government officials in Curaçao were prepared to believe, however, there was no concrete evidence that the May rebellion was sparked by communists or was directly influenced by Cuba. Yet in a sense the Cuban revolution did have a kind of indirect influence. It became a romantic symbol for many of the leading dissidents in the May Movement. For example, some of them imitated the khaki military dress made famous by Castro and his followers and rode around the island in a jeep. This practice provoked disapproval from many persons it was probably designed to bother, for example, government officials, which more than likely contributed to its continuation. Cuba was also used by some of the dissidents as a standard by which to compare circumstances in Curaçao, as in the case, for example, of the leader who suggested that Antilleans should be as free as the Cubans have been since the Castro-led revolution.

Recently in the Commonwealth Caribbean or West Indies, black power movements have been the major form that radical movements for change have assumed. Such movements have been active on such Caribbean islands as Barbados, Grenada, Saint Lucia, Jamaica, and Trinidad-Tobago. McDonald provides us with insight into the conditions that give rise to such movements in the following observation.

> The Caribbean is a beautiful "house with an African personality"; but its wealth and beauty have been the privilege and property of Europeans or North Americans for over three hundred years. And all the while, the Afro-Caribbean character of the region has been continuously exploited or oppressed. It seems inescapable that this contradiction, dehumanizing both for the oppressor and the oppressed, will have to be radically changed, one way or another.[7]

The most dramatic action by any of the black power movements took place in Trinidad from February 26 to April 22, 1970. During this period, a small activist organization called the National Joint

Action Committee led a mass movement consisting of students, unemployed blacks and East Indians, and trade union leaders in protest demonstrations against the political and economic establishment. One of the leaders voiced the goal of the movement in the following way.

> Our movement is working toward the day when each black person will be able to get a fair deal, be he of African or East Indian descent, will be able to feel that he has a stake in the future of our society. We are therefore against the present system in Trinidad which can only result in the perpetuation of the status-quo. In Trinidad we have a black Government which is not working in the interest of the people, for they strive to perpetuate a system of capitalism, a system which serves to provide huge profits for the foreign firms like the Royal Bank of Canada, Alcan, or Texaco Trinidad. We cannot and indeed will not allow our black people to be further dehumanized. And I say to you, there must be change.[8]

The movement kept Trinidad in a state of turmoil for eight weeks, with even half of the army rebelling, before the government was finally able to end the protest.

As was true of events in Cuba, the black power movements that developed in Jamaica, Barbados, and other parts of the Caribbean touched Curaçao indirectly rather than directly. There was no evidence, for example, that local dissidents in Curaçao were "advised" by black power leaders from other islands. Yet what developed in Curaçao was not isolated from happenings in the rest of the Caribbean. Dissidents in Curaçao were not unaware of what was occurring throughout the Caribbean, just as they were not unaware of the riots by ghetto residents and the black power movement in the United States. Some of the symbols, rhetoric, and issues used by May Movement protestors were similar to those associated with movements on other Caribbean islands and in the United States. Again this is understandable since Curaçao shares with other Caribbean islands and the United States problems of race and poverty, and the ease with which strategies of protest can be shared among societies given the effective means of communication and transportation available in the modern world. Seeing parallels between the May Movement and black power movements in the Caribbean and the United States, some Antillean government officials looked for an explanation in some type of conspiracy. One conspiracy "theory" that gained considerable attention in Curaçao involved a man by the name of Fox. This man was an Antillean who had spent many years in New York before returning to Curaçao sometime before the outbreak of the May 30 rebellion. In conversations around the island, Fox often used black power rhetoric and told people that he had been associated with the black power movement while living in the United States. He wore a dashiki and showed his identification with the cultural aspects of the black radical movement in other ways, such as giving the black power handshake and the clenched fist greeting symbolizing the call for black power. Because of his mode of behavior and because he arrived just before the May 30 violence, some government officials were of the opinion that he might have been sent by black power groups in the United States to organize the riot in Curaçao. However, there was no evidence to support this view. And a commission that was later appointed by the government to investigate the causes of the riot did not mention Fox as having any responsibility for the violence that took place (see Appendix B for the conclusions and some of the recommendations that appeared in the commission's report).

Although similar to the black power movements that evolved in the Caribbean and the United States around the same period, the May Movement was also different from them in many significant ways because of Curaçao's different sociohistorical background, which we will consider at some length later. Strictly speaking, the May Movement was not a black power movement. There certainly was a call for a more equitable distribution of power between the races and an end to racism in the Antilles. But the movement's basic message was a demand for greater Antillean influence over the affairs of the former Dutch colony and a new, more dignified identity to replace the one that had been badly damaged by years of Dutch colonial rule and more recently by the foreign domination of the local economy and way of life. Certainly black Antilleans were seen as those most in need of such changes in the society, but many

May Movement dissidents also felt that local whites would and should benefit from them too. Furthermore, whites were hardly excluded from participating in the May Movement. In fact, a white school teacher was one of the principal leaders of the May Movement and was largely responsible for the involvement of many teachers and intellectuals in its activities. Clearly, too, some of the dissidents were inspired by other forms of radicalism in addition to black power politics. For example, some of the teachers who participated in May Movement activities had been radicalized while attending universities in the Netherlands. For them, the student experience afforded the opportunity to associate with persons possessing different outlooks, leading in many cases to their acquiring a new political awareness and involvement in demonstrations and radical youth movements while in Holland. One young teacher and participant in the May Movement reported that she had had this kind of experience to the dismay of her parents, whom she felt had wanted her to attend a Dutch university in order to find a husband and settle down there rather than return to Curaçao. In order to combat this influence on the youth, one Antillean legislator proposed a new law that would have required that recipients of government scholarships attend college outside the Netherlands.

In summary, the May Movement arose at a time when considerable protest abound in the Caribbean and other parts of the Third World, as well as in the black ghettos of the United States and parts of Europe. Thus the May Movement reflected many of the characteristics of such protest efforts outside of the Netherlands Antilles. Still the May Movement represented a different mixture of characteristics since its participants reshaped ideas that were borrowed elsewhere to make them fit their experiences and added many new ideas of their own. These ideas will be elaborated in succeeding chapters. Now let us turn to a discussion of the mode of analysis we used in this study.

SOCIAL MOVEMENTS AND SOCIAL CHANGE

Although our initial interest in Curaçao was in the violence described above, as we attempted to understand it, we found ourselves considering the past; and as we took time to understand the past, questions came to mind regarding Curaçao's future. Thus, we became involved in a study of social change. We soon found it useful to see the violent incident as one part of a totality of collective action that we call the May Movement. We came to appreciate the importance of this social movement in the process of social change in Curaçao. Thus Turner and Killian's definition of a social movement seems adequate for the purpose of this study: "a collectivity acting with some continuity to promote or resist a change in the society or group of which it is a part."[9]

We will consider the several ways in which the May Movement was related to social change. Many of the ideas that guided us in our analysis were drawn from the growing, but still diffuse, literature on social movements.[10] Some of these ideas will be introduced before we move on to further description and analysis. We will briefly discuss (a) the relation of social movements to social strain, (b) some of the internal dynamics that characterize social movements, and (c) some of the considerations that have to be given in assessing the success of a movement.

*Social Movements and Social Strain*

Simple societies are less likely to have social movements since a certain level of complexity is required. With increasing complexity, there will be increasing heterogeneity and more diversity of viewpoints about the necessity of change. In such societies, it is more likely that people will be able to find others with similar ideas to join collectively to press for change. Too, some of the dimensions that have created the increasing complexity are likely to be productive of social strain.[11] Social and cultural conflicts, deprivations and discrepancies are the types of strain that scholars have most often associated with the rise of movements. For example, social movements are likely to develop when there is conflict between two cultures, especially when one culture threatens to dominate another. In such a case, the threatened cultural group may form a social movement to protect or to revitalize its cultural heritage. Different types of deprivations have been identified as contributing to the generation of social movements. Some groups in a society may see themselves, relative to others, as being economically oppressed. They may thus form a movement to collectively improve their economic position. Also, deprivation may be interpreted by groups in political terms. For example, the belief may be shared among certain segments of a population that they possess insufficient political power and influence. In colonial and neo-colonial societies such beliefs have served as the catalyst for the organization of nationalist movements. Discrepancies such as inconsistencies between ideal and real norms also have been identified as possible sources of pressure for change in societies. Groups that are denied rights guaranteed by their society's legal statutes may, through collective action in a social movement, attempt to close the gap between their actual experiences and the ideal norms and values specified in law. Civil rights movements represent this type of response.

As we shall see, there were various themes of protest in the May Movement that suggested that it too grew out of strains somewhat similar to those referred to above. The movement eventually addressed itself to various economic, political, and sociocultural problems in the society. And like movements generally, it emerged when more institutionalized means for bringing about desired change seemed inadquate.

In addition to preexisting strains, some major event often plays a significant role in the final crystallization of a movement. In some cases, this may be a dramatic crisis that emphasizes the need for innovative behavior or increases the opportunity for it. The riots of the 1960s in the United States, for example, were the catalyst for the formation of several new black movements. Similarly, a period of labor unrest in Curaçao and the violent incident previously described culminated in the emergence of the May Movement. Without this crisis, a serious collective effort to reduce certain strains in the society might have been longer in coming.

## Social Movement Organization and Social Change

One of the topics we will discuss is the various organizational changes the May Movement underwent. Thus it would be useful at this point to make several comments on how social movements are organized. Students of collective behavior and social movements characterize the organization or structure of social movements as being emergent in nature. Turner and Killian note, for example:

> As a collectivity, a movement is a group with indefinite and shifting membership and with leadership whose position is determined more by the informal response of the members than by formal procedures for legitimizing authority.[12]

Like other collectivities, then, a movement has a structure and a division of labor, but these tend to be less clear cut than in established groups and organizations. Typically, movements have highly dedicated cadres, or core groups, that are heavily involved in trying to reach desired goals, and larger and less committed groups of members. Usually, because of their visibility, and often charismatic appeal, certain members of the core group come to symbolize the movement to outsiders as well as insiders.

There is, however, considerable variation among social movements in the degree to which they are organized or integrated. There are some social movements with well-defined roles, mechanisms for coordination, and explicit criteria for membership. Generally, however, integration and coordination tend to be problematic. Social movements tend to be marked by considerable dissensus. As Killian has noted: "Many movements are comprised of diverse segments, each with its own structure, loosely united only by their allegiance to the central, explicit values and by the tendency of outsiders to view them as parts of a single whole."[13] In fact, the interaction between the various components of a social movement is often characterized by conflict. A case in point is the civil rights movement in the United States.

The organization of a social movement has a dynamic quality. At a later point in its history, a movement may manifest considerably more coordination and integration than it did earlier. Scholars employing a natural history model have been particularly sensitive to the possibilities for the internal transformation of movements. For example, Dawson and Gettys in their classic statement suggest that movements begin during a preliminary stage of unrest, pass through a popular stage of collective excitement into a third stage of formal organization, and finally reach a fourth stage of institutionalization.[14] Particularly relevant to our analysis is a model employed by some social scientists which suggests that movements tend to move from a low to a high degree of organization and concomitantly from a low to high degree of political awareness. For example, Oppenheimer says, "Historically, it would seem, urban mobs and riots give way to more sophisticated political forms, such as modern social movements (trade unionism, for example, or working class political parties), where such forms are feasible."[15] This kind of model of social movement transformation seems useful if a simple determinism is avoided. We will employ such a model in this study. The May Movement experienced increasing organization and politicization, and we will seek an explanation of these internal changes in factors both internal and external to the movement.

The interplay between internal consensus and conflict gives movements much of their dynamic quality. Movements are often comprised of diverse groups. Such heterogeneous components may be held together by their general agreement on goals, tactics, and ideology and by the interpersonal ties between leaders and followers. In addition to creating stability, the emergence of greater consensus within a movement may also at times produce internal change. A coalition or merger may be formed between once competing factions, and even a more inclusive social movement may be created that includes elements once considered outside the original movement.

Although the social organization of movements may change because of factors that increase consensus, it is internal conflict or dissensus that perhaps plays a more significant role in making a movement dynamic. Internal conflict and competition often lead to factions and splits within movements.[16] Indeed, such processes as conflict and competition are so ubiquitous to movements that outsiders and critics of movements are often unable to see how they can achieve their goals. In our analysis of the May Movement, we will show how internal conflict, like consensus, becomes important at certain points in the career of a movement.

What are some of the internal sources of dissensus that give movements much of their dynamic character? The ideology may be one important area of conflict. Even though various groups may generally subscribe to a common ideology, so that we can say that they are part of the same movement, there nevertheless may be disagreement over specific and even basic points, which leads to internal competition and conflict. Opposing factions may vie for recognition and the acceptance of their particular position. Dissensus may also exist within a movement over tactics and strategy. Among civil rights groups in the United States, for example, there is disagreement over the means to be employed in reaching the goal of equality for black Americans. Personal antagonisms and ambitions may also lead to factionalization and the emergence of competing elements in movements. Aspiring leaders constantly appear in movements to challenge the existing leadership. Too, groups and organizations belonging to the same movement often have links to different outside organizations. Such extramovement associations of member groups and organizations often create internal conflict within a movement. This occurs when certain segments of a movement view these associations as a potential threat to the success of the movement or when the outside group to which a member organization is linked is generally viewed in negative terms.

Quite obviously, external factors affect social movement organization. The structure of a movement may be transformed in response to environmental pressures, and in some cases the very existence and viability of a movement may be threatened by external elements. The response of groups in power to a movement, and, in particular, the response of social control agencies, is important in determining its character. Those in power may effectively defuse or can contribute to the breakup of a potentially radical movement by granting certain reforms or by coopting its leaders.[17] On the other hand, an incipient movement may be able to continue its development due to outside support.

In this study, then, we will examine both internal and external factors in accounting for the dynamics of the May Movement. Also, we will look for characteristics it shares with other movements in this regard, as well as differences.

*Social Movement Success Through Social Change*

The success of social movements has to be judged by the extent to which they are able to initiate change in society or reduce particular strains. It is not easy to determine whether a movement has succeeded or failed. The goals of movements are often stated in such vague or general terms that it may be almost impossible to measure the extent to which they have been achieved. It often becomes exceedingly difficult to credit a solution to a problem or an instance of social change to a particular movement since many movements and organizations may be operating in the same areas. Yet in spite of such problems, we do know that some social movements meet with a degree of success. In some instances this may be minor success, whereas in other cases it is major, with the movement having a profound effect upon society. Even movements that "fail" and disappear sometimes have an impact on society by spawning other movements.[18]

There are several ways in which movements may achieve success. Killian notes that third-party movements in the United States have been successful in an indirect way.

> One way in which a movement may contribute to social change is through forcing the established structure of the society to come to terms with it and its values, incorporating some features of its programs into existing institutions. This is best exemplified by the fate of "third party" movements in American history which, although failing to win political power, have at times forced major parties to adopt modified versions of their programs.[19]

A more direct way for a movement to achieve success is through revolution. Again Killian notes, "A movement which is sufficiently ambitious in terms of its goals and is strongly power-oriented may be successful in seizing control of the entire group or society—a revolution is effected. The movement is rapidly transformed into a particular type of association, a government."[20]

What determines the degree of success a movement experiences? The answer to this question lies in the character of a movement itself and the environment in which it operates. A political movement, for example, will be successful to the extent that it has power to force other groups to accede to its demands. Such power comes from the possession of valued resources: organization, finances, manpower, knowledge, and the like. Being emergent phenomena, social movements are usually quite limited by their own internal make-up, often suffering from a lack of organization, experience, and financial resources. For example, the lact of experience by those in nationalist movements has been known to be particularly limiting. In such instances, movement personnel may win political office only to find themselves still dependent upon unsympathetic administrators from the old regime who had to be retained because of their expertise. Structural conditions, vested interest groups, and countermovements can limit the success of a social movement. Thus, as we will examine in the case of the May Movement, the success of a movement in achieving its goals and initiating change in society is likely to be a function of the relative strength of facilitating and limiting forces within and outside the movement.

Many movements undergo a violent phase during their careers. Such violence often involves arson, looting, and, in some cases, even personal attacks. This kind of violence typically has a low degree of organization, but it may have implications for the ultimate success of a social movement. This possibility is often overlooked. Gary Marx, for example, chided the National Advisory Commission on Civil Disorders for not considering the "positive" consequences of the riots of the 1960s in its report.

> The Commission asserts that violence can never be a factor in bringing about change. Nevertheless in a majority of the cities it studied there was evidence of positive change following the disorders. . . . Just as Negroes taking to the streets in civil disobedience in the early 60's seemed to inspire much civil rights legislation and activity, so recent

violence has spurred great concern with what is called the "urban crisis."[21]

Violence can have an effect on both those inside and outside a movement. It may, for example, motivate those in power to try and accommodate some of the movement's demands. But perhaps even more significantly, violence may result in increasing solidarity and political awareness within the protesting group. Marx suggests that this happened in the United States following the riots in the 1960s.[22] In our analysis, we will show that a similar development occurred in Curaçao after the May 30 violence.

It is usual, however, to view violent protest as irrational and, by definition, nonproductive. The actions of hostile crowds are often seen as isolated episodes, unconnected with other events in society, and having little real purpose. However, in our conceptual framework, we will place such violent crowd outbreaks in the larger context of social movements. Geschwender sees the recent urban riots in the United States in much the same way.

> The earlier discussion of looting strongly suggested that current urban disorders were a developing part of the civil rights movement. . . . The present author no longer questions that the urban disorders are, in fact, creative rioting. Creative rioting falls clearly within the evolutionary pattern of the civil rights movement, a social movement which may or may not eventually become revolutionary.[23]

Thus crowd violence may be, in itself, a phase of a movement, less organized perhaps than other phases, but yet not necessarily irrational and without purpose. Furthermore, the nonutility of such behavior cannot be assumed since it may contribute to the success of a movement by making a social system more open to change and reform. Collective violence may also lead to the increasing organization and political sophistication of a movement, thus enabling it to more effectively pursue long-range goals. We shall examine these possibilities in Curaçao.

Our orientation regarding the relationship of social movements and social change can be summarized as follows. (1) Social movements are important to study in their own right because they are a type of social change. Thus we see them as significant events in the history of a society. Also, since they are dynamic social forms, their analysis over time, that is, the study of their careers, should provide further insight into the nature of social change. (2) We assume that the deliberate and conscious efforts of men to modify existing political, economic and social arrangements are not doomed to failure. We further assume that a movement's actions may have both manifest and latent consequences. That is, a movement may not only realize its goals and produce planned social change but may also precipitate unanticipated changes. (3) Finally, we take the position that preexisting changes and other conditions in society should be taken into account in any analysis of the relationship between social movements and social change. However, these variables should not be emphasized to the point that the internal dynamics and careers of movements and their impact on society are ignored.

In our analysis, we will first locate the emergence of the May Movement in particular preconditions and changes in Curaçao. Then we will analyze the internal dynamics of the movement. Finally, we will assess the consequences that the May Movement had for the society over a two-year period. The major questions we will seek to answer about the May Movement, in one way or another, involve the matter of social change. Why did the May Movement emerge? Did it emerge because of changes in Curaçao or because of the unwillingness of those in power to make changes desired by certain groups? Did the May Movement undergo internal changes similar to other movements? What changes, if any, did the movement initiate in the society? Was its success in achieving change limited by internal or external conditions? Through our analysis, we hope to answer these and related questions.

Curaçao has had a long and interesting history. Some understanding of it, particularly the sources of the population and the background of certain political and economic issues, are important in understanding the May Movement. The next chapter provides the initial background.

# CHAPTER TWO

# Curaçao: History and Development

To some, Curaçao is a quaint stop on the Caribbean cruise circuit and is remembered for being a bit of Holland, since this impression is given by the architecture around the port at Willemstad. The shops downtown contain a cornucopia of items for the transient traveler to purchase. Some pick up a bottle of the locally made liqueur and go back to their ship to be off to another exotic island. Others who stay longer remember Curaçao for its hotels—the Intercontinental nesting within the walls of the old fort, the lavish Hilton, the Flamboyant Beach, and now the inevitable Holiday Inn. To others, because of its oil industry, Curaçao may give the appearance of a technological monster—a mass of intertwined pipes, oil storage tanks, tankers, and gas burn-off torches, which eerily illuminate the night. All of these manifestations are the result of a long and interesting history.

Curaçao's history involves people whose fame came elsewhere, such as Amerigo Vespucci, who wrote about Curaçao as being an "Isle of Giants," and Peter Stuyvesant, who left a leg (sometimes rumored to be buried in Curaçao) in the Caribbean before he went on to what was to become New York. Spanish buccaneers sailed the waters around the island as did German U-boats several hundred years later. The British captured it and Venezuelan revolutionaries almost did a century later. Until 1825, it was the site

1. *Netherlands Antilles 1969 Statistical Yearbook* (Willemstad: Bureau of Statistics, 1969), p. 23.

2. *Amigoe di Curaçao,* May 31, 1969.

3. *Investment Factors: Netherlands Antilles* (Willemstad: Department of Social and Economic Affairs, 1965), p. 30.

4. *Amigoe di Curaçao,* May 31, 1969.

5. Edward A. de Jongh, *May 30, 1969: The Most Historic Day* (Willemstad: Privately published, 1969).

6. *New York Times,* September 21, 1962. Copyright© 1962 by the New York Times Company. Reprinted by permission.

7. Frank McDonald, "The Commonwealth Carribbean," in *The United States and the Caribbean,* ed. Tad Szulc. Copyright© 1971 by the American Assembly, Columbia University. Published by Prentice-Hall, Inc., Englewood Cliffs, New Jersey. Used by permission.

8. Geddes Granger, quoted in Ibid., p. 164.

9. Ralph Turner and Lewis Killian, *Collective Behavior* (Englewood Cliffs, N.J.: Prentice Hall, Inc., 1972), p. 246.

10. For a review of this literature, see, in addition to Turner and Killian's book: Anthony Oberschall, *Social Conflict and Social Movements* (Englewood Cliffs, N.J.: Prentice Hall, Inc., 1973); Gary B. Rush and R. Serge Denisoff, *Social and Political Movements* (New York: Appleton-Century-Crofts, 1971); and John Wilson, *Introduction to Social Movements* (New York; Basic Books, 1973).

11. Those familiar with Smelser's theory of collective behavior will recognize that we have collapsed his "structural conduciveness" and "structural strain" together here. Neil J. Smelser, *Theory of Collective Behavior* (New York: The Free Press, 1962).

12. Turner and Killian, *Collective Behavior,* p. 246.

13. Lewis Killian, "Social Movements" in *Handbook of Modern Sociology,* ed. R. E. Faris (Chicago: Rand McNally, 1964), p. 440. Used by permission.

14. C. A. Dawson and W. E. Gettys, *An Introduction to Sociology* (New York: Ronald Press, 1948), p. 690.

15. Martin Oppenheimer, *The Urban Guerrilla* (Chicago: Quadrangle Press, 1969), p. 37.

16. Mayer Zald and Roberta Ash, "Social Movements: Growth, Decay and Change," *Social Forces* 44 (March, 1966):327–40.

17. Oppenheimer, *The Urban Guerrilla,* p. 167.

18. Killian, "Social Movements," p. 452.

19. Ibid., p. 453.

20. Ibid.

21. Gary Marx, "Report of the National Commission: The Analysis of Disorder or Disorderly Analysis?" (paper presented at the 1968 meeting of the American Political Science Association), p. 8.

22. Ibid., p. 9.

23. James Geschwender, "Civil Rights Protest and Riots: A Disappearing Distinction," *Social Science Quarterly* 49 (December, 1968):484.

of the largest Jewish community in the Americas. It is the site of the oldest synagogue in the Western hemisphere, founded in 1654, and the oldest Jewish cemetery, in 1659. Curaçao also became an important slave depot, which supplied the Spanish colonies and other customers. Later, Curaçao, with the Shell refinery, supplied most of the fuel oil used by the Allies during World War II.

From this overview, one can see that Curaçao's history is long and complex.[1] It encompasses invasion, colonization, slavery, recruitment of an industrial labor force, as well as different streams of racial and religious groups. Some background in three important areas is provided here: (1) the sources of the island's population and how these sources affected the dimensions of class, status, and power in the development of the stratification system; (2) the island's economic history, with emphasis on the building of the refinery and the role of the labor unions; and (3) the island's semiautonomous status in the Kingdom of the Netherlands and the role of political parties in island politics. This information will provide some understanding of how this Spanish cattle ranch became an island "kept afloat by oil."

POPULATION SOURCES

Since the Arawak Indians were ultimately poor historians, we do not know their reaction to their "discovery" on Curaçao by one of Columbus's lieutenants in 1499. Amerigo Vespucci was a member of this expedition and must have been impressed since he wrote about an "Isle of Giants." If his description was aimed toward stimulating interest, for home consumption, it did not attract immediate attention since it was not until 1527 that the Spanish colonized the island and placed it under the control of the governor of Coro in Venezuela. The Spanish subsequently used the island as a cattle ranch and did little to defend or develop it.

Holland, at the end of the sixteenth century, needed a trade outlet for the business that had been made possible by the growth of her naval forces. The success of the Dutch East India Company led to the formation of a similar company to exploit the West Indies. In 1621, the Dutch West India Company was organized and received a monopoly of trade on the west coast of Africa and the eastern coasts of the Americas. The charter gave the company all the rights of sovereignty usually reserved to political states. It gave the company control of the slave trade in this territory.

In 1634, a 400-man expedition from the company occupied Curaçao with little opposition. The Spanish surrendered on the condition that the garrison—32 Spanish and 450 Indians—be transported to Venezuela. The Dutch, by their conquest, came into possession of an island that had several excellent harbors to assist them in their effort to harass Spanish shipping. They fortified the island. Large warehouses and slave pens were built and gradually the island became a transshipment port for great quantities of sugar, cocoa, and tobacco. In 1635, there were 412 Europeans (almost all military personnel) and 50 Indians.

In 1642, Peter Stuyvesant came to the island as director. There are indications that he did not like the island and he recommended to the company that the island be abandoned. His opinion toward the area was probably not enhanced when he lost his leg on one of his various expeditions outside the island. When his authority was expanded to include New Netherlands, he left Curaçao in 1647 to go north where he gained lasting fame. He continued to administer Curaçao from there for the next seventeen years and the North American colony furnished Curaçao with food while the island supplied some slaves, salt, and horses.

Just prior to the time that Stuyvesant came to Curaçao, the company had seriously considered giving private individuals the right to colonize and trade freely in Curaçao. Even with the growth of the slave trade, the company realized that not even a profitable slave trade could provide a stable economy by itself and that colonists and tradesmen would be needed.

### Protestant Dutchmen

The company sent Protestant Dutchmen and other northwestern Europeans as employees of the company. Some other immigrants from the same sources were attracted by what was going on in the

Caribbean or were attracted by various inducements offered for colonization. These migrants set the tone for the island based on reproducing the Netherlands as they remembered it. In house construction and dress, they made few concessions to the differences in climate. Although these white Protestants represented some diversity in their class origins in Europe, their small number and their common heritage inhibited initially the development of status differences.

*Sephardic Jews*

In Amsterdam at that time were many Jews who had earlier fled Portugal as a consequence of the Inquisition. Many of these Jews were now involved in various aspects of life in Holland. In fact, the interpreter (and thus an officer) on the original company expedition was a Jew. In 1651, a contract was let with the company to establish a Jewish colony on Curaçao. This contract calling for fifty colonists was only to produce twelve. Another contract was let the following year but it is unlikely that this group even reached the island. Faced with these failures, the company decided to increase its inducements for colonization. In particular, Stuyvesant's reluctance to sell slaves to the colonists was seen as forcing potential settlers to Barbados and other islands where they could buy slaves.

When the Dutch abandoned Brazil in 1654, a number of Jews who had gone there returned to Amsterdam. One of the earlier settlers in Brazil, Da Costa, was willing to try again and no doubt had heard of previous attempts to settle Curaçao. Da Costa's father was a prominent member of the Portuguese Jewish community in Amsterdam, and he probably had known the new governor in Curaçao who had previously served in Brazil. Da Costa was able to gather some twelve families (about seventy people) to go to Curaçao in 1659. These families were the progenitors of the current Portuguese families who still live on the island. Da Costa's privileges were superior to the previous contracts. The Jewish community could receive help from the local government in disciplining their members. They could buy slaves and build houses. They were given two miles of land and other assistance from the governor.

Although the initial intent of those who were recruited to come to Curaçao was farming, farming was risky business. The soil was not as productive as most other Caribbean islands. Droughts were frequent and water was in short supply. Certain types of enterprises, for example, cattle-breeding and cattle-trading, were a monopoly of the company. Many of the earlier residents became involved in supplying the company with everything necessary for its garrision and its slaves. The "success" of the slave trade meant that provisions increasingly had to be sought outside the island through trade.

The Jewish families did particularly well in this commerce since they had dependable representatives, generally relatives, in Amsterdam and in other cities. In addition, many of them had linguistic skills and knowledge of the Caribbean area derived from their previous experience in Brazil. Later in 1674 when the company allowed it, some of the merchants did enter the slave trade. With trade of all kinds, it is not surprising that Jews also entered into the shipping field, as owners and as charterers of ships. By 1715, they had practical control of most of the commerce and navigation on the island. At that time there were probably 425 white families and 3,500 slaves, excluding those owned by the company; the Jews represented about 35 percent of the white population. From 1726 to 1770, the Jews outnumbered the rest of the white population.[2]

The Protestant Dutchmen and the Sephardic Jews were in a certain sense the original residents of Curaçao since almost all of the native Indians had left with the Spanish and those who remained were absorbed into the general population. The two "white" sources, however, did not mold together but each maintained their distinctiveness. They were different not only in origin but also in religion and language. Their growing occupational differentiation reinforced the initial differences. The Dutch and Jews also lived in different parts of Willemstad, separated by water. These forms of distinctiveness were further reinforced by intramarriage. The Jews managed to exercise control in these areas by the greater cohesiveness of their community.

In the first century and a half after Dutch capture, classes did develop particularly among the Protestants. A local aristocracy evolved from the higher civil servants, military personnel, and prosperous merchants. The local status symbol—the acquisition of a plantation, a country house—was a mark of belonging to the aristocracy. Since these plantations were not particularly economically productive, they functioned more as a symbol of conspicuous consumption. A lower class of white Protestants also developed composed of those in the retail trades and crafts as well as the captains of the sailing vessels so necessary to the trade of the island. Among the aristocratic Protestants in particular, a close identification was claimed to the Netherlands and especially to Amsterdam. This was evidenced by the fact that many of the shutters on the houses were painted red and black in the colors of the city of Amsterdam. Curaçao was a Caribbean extension of the Netherlands.

### Negro Slaves

One of the original purposes of the company was to develop the slave trade. Since the Spanish colonies had a shortage of labor, the Spanish king used to contract with a merchant an asiento—a contract of delivery for the exclusive right to import slaves. Since Spain did not want to invest the vast sums necessary, merchants from Amsterdam supplied much of the funding for such contracts. For 130 years, starting in 1648, slaves were imported to Curaçao. The majority of them, however, were eventually sold to surrounding countries. The long trip across the Atlantic and its consequences for the health of the slaves required some "storage" facilities on the island. Two slave camps were built where as many as 15,000 slaves were located at one time. During the period of contract with Spain, 4,000 slaves had to be supplied a year. The peak years were from 1685 to 1713. In subsequent years, the number declined to perhaps 500 to 600 a year in 1750. The majority of slaves came from what now constitutes Ghana and the area surrounding it. The last slave ship docked in 1778; the slave trade was forbidden in 1818; and in 1863 slavery was abolished.

In addition to being a way station for the Spanish contract, some of the slaves were also retained by the company and others were sold to plantation owners and others on the island. There are indications that master-slave relations on Curaçao were relatively tranquil. Many of the slaves on the plantations were in effect house slaves since the plantations often had little field work. Compared with slavery systems in other Caribbean countries of the time period, it is likely that Curaçao was somewhat less harsh. Local legislation was passed governing the treatment of slaves. For example, in 1824 an ordinance was passed that limited the slave's work day to ten hours. (In Europe at that same time, factory workers had just been limited to a twelve-hour day.) There were, however, two minor slave uprisings in 1750 and 1795, the last a spillover from uprisings in Haiti.

Not all Negroes stayed slaves. Slaves were periodically freed. Sometimes the motives for freeing slaves were not necessarily charitable. Slavery placed obligations of "care" on the part of the masters, as the previously mentioned legislation suggests. Some of the slave owners obviated their obligations by freeing slaves who were old or not economically productive. To check the abuse of manumission, the company levied a fee. But by 1816, there were 2,781 whites, 4,003 colored freemen, and 6,026 slaves. (In some British Caribbean possessions at that time, there were 10 slaves for every freeman.)

In 1850, manumission fees were abolished and an increasing number of slaves were set free. Many of these slaves when they were freed were given names that identified them with their previous owners. For example, Jesurun was altered to Zurun, Leon was changed to de Leeuw, Schotborgh to Borghschot, Ellis to Sille. Government slaves were given names such as Ven den Lande (of the government). Others were named after their plantation, for example, Hato and Rosentak. From 1851 to 1862, 1,062 manumissions took place. Finally in July, 1863, the remaining slaves, over 6,700, were given their freedom. More than two-thirds of these had been employed on various plantations. Many of them continued to work on these plantations as domestics and field hands. Some left the island, but others later settled down on land obtained when the government bought and parceled out some of the former plantations.

The social distance between whites and blacks that was rooted in slavery was reinforced further by religious differences. The Protestant aristocracy was almost uniformly Dutch Reformed, again symbolic of its ties to the mother country. Rather than encourage the assimilation of large numbers of blacks to this faith, they allowed Catholic missionaries to come to the island with the implicit responsibility of "Christianizing" the blacks.

## Colored

Even though a superordinate-subordinate relationship existed continuously between white and black, the long and continued contact between the two groups led, in time, to the creation of an intermediate colored group, separate from the other two groups. Actual data on interracial alliances are, as one might expect, scanty, although the ultimate results within the population are visibly obvious. Very early in the history of Curaçao, on several different occasions, Protestant families petitioned the states of Holland and West Friesland (which had interests in the company) to forbid intermarriage between whites and mulattos, unless there was prior consent of the white parents concerned. In 1656 there was introduced a law that compelled a white person to obtain his parent's permission before he could marry a colored person. There were also attempts to secure legislation to annul intermarriages between whites and mulattos.

In addition to marriages, there were, of course, extensive extralegal relationships. One governor who had been on Curaçao for thirty-four years wrote in his report to his superiors in 1773 that: "It is generally well known throughout the world that wherever there are colonies and slaves, it is impossible to adhere to European morality with relation to marriage, but that members (of society) live in concubinage with their slaves . . . in spite of ourselves we must tolerate this situation in our own homes if we wish to be served by slaves. If we wish to change this, it will be necessary for the ministers (of religion) to be the first to clean their homes.'' Another source suggested that ''in 1788 there were not more than six white families who did not have illegitimate colored relatives.''[3]

The increasing complexity of Curaçao's racial structure was reflected in the reorganization of the National Guard in 1821. Although Jews earlier had served as a separate company, it was reorganized into five companies—Caucasians, Jews, mestizos, mulattos, and Negroes.[4] The colored category was a heterogeneous one, both physically and culturally. The guard reorganization recognized two intermediate racial categories—mestizos and mulattos. Culturally some of these colored looked toward the Netherlands as a cultural ''home'' as did the white Protestants whereas others spoke Spanish and identified themselves with South America, seeking marriage partners there. In these and other ways, they sought to minimize their identification with the blacks.

In summary, the basic structure of Curaçao toward the end of the nineteenth century consisted of: (1) an upper-status group of white, Dutch Protestants emphasizing family origins, contact with the mother country, Calvinism, governmental position, and the superiority of that which was white and European. (2) Parallel to this Dutch status group were the upper-status Sephardic Jews. They had gained economic wealth but continued to speak Portuguese and Spanish, remained in their synagogues, and emphasized their own version of culture. Their marginal position was indicated by the fact that even when they constituted the majority of whites on the island, they were treated officially as a ''Portuguese Nation.'' About the same time as the slaves were emancipated, public offices were opened to Jews (and to Catholics). In return, the Jews began to use the Dutch language in their synagogues.

In contrast to the bifurcated upper segment was the black under class. Its tenuous economic position as a consequence of the long history of slavery changed little with emancipation except for the removal of objective legal barriers. Although the blacks were perhaps compensated psychologically by their conversion to Catholicism, this too tended to reinforce their inferior position.

In between were the colored and the lower Protestants, their ancestry making them superior to blacks. Both the colored and the lower Protestants were not accepted by the upper class, particularly the Dutch Protestants, and they did not identify down. They were often forced into an identification with pseudo-Dutchness or with South America. In 1914, there were about 4,000 whites (including about 1,000 Jews) and about 26,000 Negroes and colored.

### THE IMPACT OF THE REFINERY ON CURAÇAO

During the nineteenth century, Curaçao suffered economically and politically. It was no longer particularly important within the Dutch empire. The slave trade was coming to an end and Indonesia was attracting more attention from the Netherlands. During this time people on Curaçao lived by trade and by the shipping connected with it. There were some small profits to be made in dye-wood and in salt, but the major domestic industry, the manufacture of straw hats, had to depend on straw that was imported.

At the beginning of the twentieth century, one writer's description of Curaçao as being a losing colonial venture was appropriate. He said "Curaçao will in time be obliged to yield to the inevitable and take the place that her geographic and climatic conditions have ordained—a lonely island with little political or commercial importance and a small and poor population. . . . Curaçao assumed an importance which will . . . soon be little more than a memory."[5]

These dismal expectations, however, changed rapidly within the next several years. The opening of the Panama Canal made it seem likely that Curaçao would become an important refueling port and improvements were made in the harbor in 1912 with such expectations. The discovery of oil in and around Lake Maracaibo

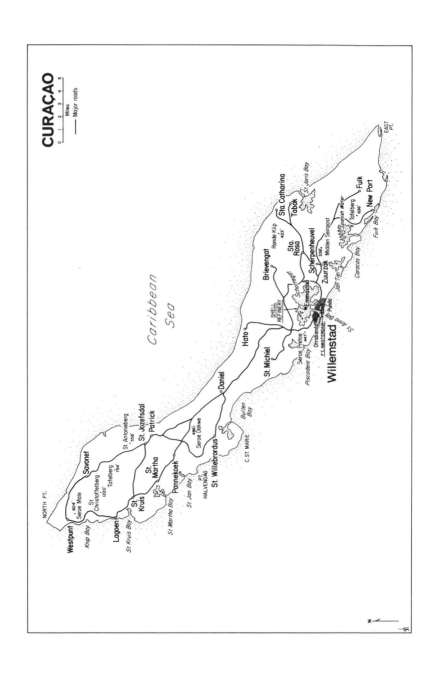

in Venezuela prompted the Shell Oil Company to establish a refinery to process this crude oil. In 1915, the construction started, and, in 1918, the plant was put into operation and continued to expand until 1930. A second period of expansion began and continued to its peak period in 1952, when about 11,000 were employed by Shell Curaçao. During the initial period, inhabitants of Surinam, the West Indies, and Madeira were employed as contract laborers. Many came from other islands in the Antilles. Dutchmen came from the Netherlands as civil servants, technicians, and as independent professionals. Eastern European and Askenazian Jews, Lebanese, Chinese, and East Indians entered the retail trades.

In addition to the influx of migrants, the economic impact of the refinery affected the traditional segments of Curaçao somewhat differentially. The Jews, mainly merchants, benefited from the economic renewal. On the other hand, the influence of the refinery was not particularly favorable to the high Protestants. New civil servants, coming from Europe, some with "modern" technical and professional skills, moved into expanded and sometimes superior governmental positions. They brought an increase in Dutch-oriented education, the use of Dutch, and contact with the home country. This influx led to internal criticism of the colonial government in the Netherlands and strengthened the in-group feeling among the Protestants on Curaçao. The term *landskind*, or native, came to be used as a mark of differentiation as did *makamba*, or European Dutchman. This in-group feeling produced a partial rapprochement between the higher and lower Protestants and among the more privileged of the colored population. The colored, having had access to better educational opportunities, tended to benefit from the impact of the refinery since it increased their employment opportunities in both government and in the private sector. In their reaction to the new migrants, the traditional white element found that though they had in the past considered Curaçao as a mere extension of the Netherlands, they had been greatly transformed over the years into something quite different. This gradual awakening of their different identity was expressed in a number of ways—a greater emphasis on the local language, Papiamento, increased pressure toward political independence, a greater emphasis on an Antillean identity, and the like.

For the blacks, the refinery did not alter their subordinate position. Although jobs were available, the blacks lacked many of the technical skills that were necessary in the new technology and outsiders were brought in for the jobs that required greater skill and training. The subordinate position of the blacks was thus continued, and their lack of skills could be used as a continued justification for their inferior position.

The impact of the building of the refinery was, of course, important in other ways. The large number of Shell employees required housing, so Shell housing estates, such as Emmastad, Julianadorp, and Bullenbaai, were built. In addition to housing, Shell also had to make other provisions, since rural Curaçao of the twenties offered few amenities. Because of a lack of water, tankers were used to bring river water from the Thames and Seine on their return trips from Europe. This water was used for gardens so that other better quality water could be used in other ways. Shell also made provisions for health care, education, and recreation. In addition, the company had to concern itself with the supply of food and other commodities as well as setting up subsidiary industries, such as docking facilities. In effect, the circumstances necessitated the development of, and perhaps more accurately the continuation of, a paternalistic system.

With the refinery, other innovations of more modern industrial systems were introduced, such as unionization. Labor relations, however, were quite peaceful during the period of expansion of the refinery. Two minor strikes, one in 1924 and the other in 1928, occurred but both involved outside workers and issues that were only tangentially economic. Unlike many other industrializing countries, there were no regulations that prevented unionism in Curaçao. A strike in 1936 did lead to the establishment of a contract committee for Shell workers. This contract committee, however, was nominated by the management and not elected by the workers, whom they were supposed to represent. In 1942, those workers with Netherlands nationality did get the right to elect a Workers Advisory Committee.

Over the years, both sides found a number of objectionable features in the existing system of representation. In 1952, the Workers Advisory Committee was divided into two bodies: (1) a Workers Council that was to represent the interests of workers in the matter of wages and labor disputes; and (2) District Representatives who were to deal with complaints and grievances. Soon the distinction between the collective and individual problems of workers proved difficult to make and the Workers Council took over all duties. Although this council was elected, it had only an advisory function and was not able to use other means, such as a strike threat or the support of fellow unionists, to implement its suggestions. On the other hand, wage scales within the oil industry were comparatively high for the Caribbean area and workers were certainly better off than they had been in years past. The presence of large refineries, such as were found on both Aruba and Curaçao, soon drew the attention of international unionism.

With the help of the CIO, Puerto Rican section, early in 1955 the Petroleum Workers Federation of Curaçao was formed. The company argued that the possibility of future strike action by the unions might cause the Venezuelan government to enter the refinery business, but the PWFC continued its unionization and demanded it be recognized as the representative of the crews on the tankers of the Curaçao Shipping Company. An election was held in 1956, and 73 percent of these workers voted for recognition. The next year, a collective agreement was worked out. On the basis of that success, the PWFC asked for a referendum among the workers at the refinery to decide whether they wished to be represented by the Workers Council or by the Federation. Seventy-one percent voted for the union. In December, 1957, a collective agreement was reached and was extended three times in 1960, 1962, and 1964.

Although the labor force at the refinery tended to dominate the total labor market in Curaçao, there were other groups for which governmental attention seemed important. In 1946, there was an ordinance regulating hours and working conditions of the steve-dores. Also in 1946, the government took on the task of setting minimum wages for certain workers, and certain mechanisms were set up to try to deal with labor disputes. Unionization in other industries led to strikes of bakers, dock workers, and workers of the phosphate company in the late 40s and 50s. Further details ·about the activities of the various unions will be presented in the next chapter.

CURAÇAO'S PLACE WITHIN THE KINGDOM OF THE
NETHERLANDS

As the previous discussion has indicated, Curaçao's relation-ship with the Netherlands has changed over time. These changes have been due to the evolution of economic and political life in both the Netherlands and in Curaçao. Curaçao has gone from an isolated property of the Dutch West India Company to colonial status, which came increasingly under parliamentary control, and finally in 1954, to a locally autonomous part of the Kingdom of the Netherlands. Also during that time, Curaçao shifted from an important economic base for the company to an economic burden within a declining empire and back again to an important economic asset with the building of the refinery. All of these changes have occurred in the context of changing ideas about the nature and scope of government, representation, and relations of colonial possessions. A brief summary of these changes are indicated below.

*Company and Colonial Dependency*

Curaçao was an outpost of the Dutch West India Company. Initially the Dutch West India Company had both political as well as economic power. The Dutch Federal Republic of the Seven Provinces entrusted the company with the administration of its American possessions. Although the company operated with pri-vate capital, its decisions were made by a board of nineteen members representing the shareholders of the various cities and provinces. The board nominated the governor and the chief magistrate in each colony. These magistrates along with three or four citizens formed the council of the colony. The dual character of the company placed a governor in an ambiguous position. The board often charged him with neglecting his commercial duties and the citizens often charged him with being too eager to make profits and in neglecting his political duties. The company existed until 1674 when it was reorganized again with more limited powers but with the same name; the new company existed until 1791.

After 1792, the administration of the colonies fell under the direct control of the Dutch government. This was a period of governmental turmoil in Europe. The federated provincial system that had operated in the Netherlands for some time was beginning to break down. It had led to indecisiveness. For this and other reasons, the dominance of Holland on the world scene had begun to dissipate. Even though the Dutch had been influenced by the democratic ideas of the French Revolution, they abandoned the idea of a republic and established a kingdom. The power of the kingdom was reflected in changes in colonial administration. Instead of the various boards and councils, the administration of the colonies and possessions became an exclusive royal prerogative. The king could not delegate these powers to a company or to a parliament, and colonial officials were responsible to the king and received their orders from him. The king, William 1, did take an interest in both the economic development and the political life of Curaçao in attempting to revive the Netherland's declining empire. Curaçao reciprocated this attention by naming its capital city Willemstad.

*Parliamentary Rule and Representation*

Democratic currents in Europe did eventually have their impact on Holland. Constitutional revision in Holland in 1848 reduced the royal power in favor of parliamentary rule and these changes affected the overseas possessions. In 1865, the Netherlands decided that the Antilles as well as Surinam should have colonial parliaments. There were interesting differences, however. While Surinam had a colonial parliament of thirteen members, nine of whom were elected by some 800 eligible voters, the Netherlands Antilles parliament had no elected members at all. In Curaçao some members were there by virtue of their offices whereas the others were appointed by the governor. The Dutch legislative assembly protested this inconsistency but finally passed the government's proposal. There were perhaps some logical as well as political reasons for such differential treatment. There were 13,000 people on the other Antillean islands in addition to the 20,000 on Curaçao, and equitable representation for a parliament would have been difficult to set up. Too, communication among the six islands was difficult at that time. Since the right to vote was then based on property considerations, only some 200 in Curaçao would have met the qualifications. Although there were some minor objections raised in Curaçao to the differential treatment in the selection of the parliament, it is likely that few in Curaçao wanted to challenge the Dutch government at that time. The islands in the Netherlands Antilles, unsuitable for extensive agricultural development, with the loss of the slave trade were now economically dependent on and nonproductive for the Dutch, who thus directed their attention toward the East Indies.

Some years later, an argument surfaced that probably had been unstated when the issue of voting in Curaçao was debated in Dutch government circles in the 1860s. In 1895 there was a debate about the problem of suffrage if election of the representatives to the colonial council were allowed. Hamelberg, a Protestant historian, was skeptical of either a propertied electorate or an electorate of the masses. Under the first system the Jews, then numbering about 850 and the wealthiest of the population, would control the colonial council. This was bad, he argued, because the Jews were not tied by "blood or history" to the Netherlands. Under an electorate of the masses, the colored population would dominate and Curaçao would become a "second Haiti." Hamelberg was opposed in his views by Abraham Chumaceiro, a lawyer and the son of a famous Curaçao rabbi. He argued that the Curaçao Jews were tied to Holland and that there were no more wealthy Jews in Curaçao than Protestants. (He forgot to mention that at that time proportionately there were then almost three times as many Protestants as Jews.) He also argued that the colored race was not inferior. He then suggested a system of voting based on property, or more correctly, monthly rental qualifications. Hamelberg responded that there were actually only a few Jewish families following Dutch customs and, invoking "proof" from English historians, he asserted that Negroes were obviously inferior. He concluded that only a Dutch administration could be neutral for the colony. This bond between Jewish wealth and the numerically dominant colored groups would seem to have effectively postponed even gradual concessions to suffrage. It was not until 1937 that the people in Curaçao got the right to vote. Even then, it was restricted, and it was not until 1948 that it was granted to all men and women.

## The Move for Greater Independence – The Charter

The building of the refinery had many noneconomic implications. The increased economic independence created the desire for greater self-government. In 1936, the Dutch government revised the regulations for the Netherlands Antilles, which led to rather paradoxical results. The Antillean government got more autonomy in local matters since the governor was given more autonomy, but, on the other hand, there was no corresponding increase in authority to the colonial parliament. The new regulations did allow for the election of a majority of the seats in the parliament by a limited electorate. This stimulated the development of some local political parties. Most of the political activity was directed toward criticizing the kingdom for its ineffective revisions.

The effectiveness of this criticism, however, was destroyed by the outbreak of World War II. The Netherlands were invaded. When Queen Wilhelmina moved her government in exile to London in 1942, she made a radio speech to the peoples of the kingdom thanking them for their support in resisting the invasion. She promised that after the war was over, steps would be taken toward a new partnership within the kingdom in which the several countries would "participate with the complete self-reliance and freedom of conduct for each part regarding its internal affairs but with the readiness to render mutual assistance." When the war was over, this goal was delayed. Indonesia was moving toward independence and had absorbed Dutch West Guinea in the process. The disintegration of the empire, however, brought Dutch attention back to the West Indies and increased their efforts to work out a satisfactory relationship with Surinam and the Netherlands Antilles. From 1946 until 1954, the reconstruction of the Dutch kingdom was completed with the issuance of a new charter.[6]

The charter was a complicated document. It tried to make possible, within the framework of a sovereign state, for two separate countries located four thousand miles from the Netherlands to have a maximum degree of autonomy. The eventual format developed is expressed on three different levels—the kingdom government, the government of the Netherlands Antilles, and the governments of the respective islands within the Netherlands Antilles. Starting with the kingdom government, the king reigns over the kingdom and over each of the countries. There is also a Council of Ministers composed of the Netherlands ministers together with the ministers plenipotentiary appointed by the Netherlands Antilles and Surinam. When a matter concerning the Netherlands Antilles or Surinam comes before the Dutch cabinet, the respective minister has the right to participate on an equal footing with the others. Foreign affairs and defense remain as kingdom matters. A governor-general represents the kingdom government in the Netherlands Antilles.

In those areas not deemed to be kingdom matters, the Netherlands Antilles became autonomous under the charter. The Netherlands Antilles government is based on a parliament called the Staten which has twenty-two members, all elected by universal suffrage of men and women from twenty-one-years old in the six islands. The members of the Staten are elected by party lists in a system of proportional representation. Curaçao elects twelve members, Aruba eight, Bonaire one, and the three Windward Islands together elect one member. This legislative body has the power to establish budgets and to propose new bills. The members may also question the cabinet. The cabinet consists of not more than seven ministers headed by a prime minister. The ministers are nominated by the governor after consultation with the parliament and ultimately are responsible to the parliament rather than the governor.

In addition to the government of the Netherlands Antilles there are also island governments. Curaçao had always held a special place within the Antilles. It was the site of the central government historically and, since it has the largest population, has tended to dominate the other islands. To mitigate this one-island domination, each of the islands, except the three Windward Islands that were bound together by one administrative unit, has its own legislative body, its own administrative council, and its own governor (a lieutenant governor). In the island governments, there is a close relationship between the legislative body and the executive body. The local governor is the actual chairman of the legislative body as well as of the executive council. The members of the council also may be members of the legislative body.

Several further comments are necessary about the political process. Although universal suffrage was instituted rather late in the political history of the Netherlands Antilles, elections have created widespread interest in the political process. Not only are elections rather exciting times but usually more than 90 percent of the electorate actually vote. The system of proportional representation used has led to the development of a multiparty system. Given this multiparty system, a one-party cabinet is exceptional. The parliamentary majority supporting the cabinet usually consists of two or more parties. The parties themselves are often coalitions of small island organizations. This means that elections are not just the result of preelection compromises; often after the election a considerable period of time can be consumed trying to work out the "best" majority. We will deal with some of the dimensions of these political dynamics in the next chapter.

In summary, Curaçao's history has involved "discovery," invasion, being an outpost of the Dutch West India Company, becoming an important link in the slave trade for Latin America, and later becoming a focal point for refining oil. As a result, the population sources of Curaçao reflect these various time periods. Sephardic Jews came to seek refuge and opportunity. Protestant Dutchmen came in administrative roles and again much later as technicians during industrialization. Slaves came, most of them for a short time, but some were retained. Later when slavery ended, those who remained became most important numerically. After a century of neglect and stagnation within the Dutch colonial empire, oil made Curaçao important again. New population elements came to build the refinery and to work in it or in the enterprises associated with refining. Curaçao was rapidly thrust into the modern industrial world, with its benefits and its tensions. With greater affluence, issues relating to Curaçao's relationship to the kingdom reemerged and new solutions were sought to deal with representation and political structure. These were elements of the heritage of Curaçao that were important in the development of the May Movement. In the next chapter, we bring together some of the more contemporary factors and issues that were significant in understanding the emergence of the May Movement in 1969.

1. The basic historical source in English is J. Hartog, *Curaçao: From Colonial Dependence to Autonomy* (Aruba: De Wit, Inc., 1968). For a specialized history, see Isaac S. and Suzanne A. Emmanuel, *History of the Jews of the Netherlands Antilles,* vol. 1, History, vol. 2, Appendixes (Cincinnati: American Jewish Archives, 1970). For a somewhat delimited view of World War II in Curaçao, see Philip Hanson Hiss, *Netherlands America: The Dutch Territories in the West* (New York: Duell, Sloan and Pearce, 1943). Other more specialized aspects can be found in Albert Gastmann, "The Charter of the Kingdom of the Netherlands"; Albert Gastmann, "The Politics of the Netherlands Antilles"; and F. M. Andic and S. Andic, "The Economy of the Netherlands Antilles"; in *Politics and Economics in the Caribbean,* ed. T. G. Mathews and F. M. Andic (Rio Piedras: Institute of Caribbean Studies, 1971). For a more dated view, see Hans G. Herman, "Constitutional Development of the Netherlands Antilles and Surinam"; J. J. Ochse, "Economic Factors in the Netherlands Antilles and Surinam"; and Andre L. van Assendorp, "Some Aspects of Society in the Netherlands Antilles and Surinam"; in *The Caribbean: British, Dutch, French, United States,* ed. A. Curtis Wilgus (Gainesville: University of Florida Press, 1958).

2. The Jewish community on Curaçao is significant for reasons other than their long history of involvement on the island. Many American Jewish families of today, such as the Maduros, Firdanques, Delvalles, and Jesurun Lindos can trace their ancestry back to those who emigrated from Curaçao to New York toward the close of the nineteenth century. The Jewish community also provided financial assistance to many new Jewish communities elsewhere. In 1729, assistance was given toward the construction of Sherith Israel Synagogue in New York. In 1764, it contributed toward the payment of a debt on the oldest synagogue now surviving in the United States—Touro Synagogue of Newport, Rhode Island. In this, they had special interest since Ishac Touro had emigrated from Curaçao to North America in 1693 and the synagogue was named for his son. In addition to this emigration to North America, Jews who left Curaçao settled in Santo Domingo (Dominican Republic), Venezuela (Coro and Maricaibo), Saint Thomas, and Costa Rica. Almost all of the Jews living in Panama have Curaçao ancestors.

3. Emmanuel and Emmanuel, *History of the Jews of the Netherlands Antilles,* 1:145.

4. Ibid., 2:1075.

5. Herdman F. Cleland, "Curaçao, A Losing Colonial Venture," *Bulletin of the American Geographical Society* 41, no. 3 (1909):138.

6. Charter for the Kingdom of the Netherlands (The Hague: Vice Prime Minister's Cabinet Department, n.d.). The charter is always subject to change. As a result of discussions between Dutch and Surinamese officials during the middle seventies, it is expected that Surinam will become totally independent from the Netherlands by 1976. The status of the Netherlands Antilles will remain basically the same, at least for the near future.

# CHAPTER THREE

## The Contemporary Scene: Social Change
## And the Response to Social Strain

Having provided a broad outline of the history of Curaçao in Chapter two, we are now prepared to turn to more recent developments in the society. In spite of Curaçao's early history, the May Movement might not have evolved had it not been for more recent changes in the society involving such aspects as politics and economics. Such developments were necessary ingredients for the emergence of the May Movement.

### THE POPULATION BASE AND THE STRATIFICATION SYSTEM

During the nineteenth century, Curaçao's economic stagnation forced many persons to leave, but the discovery of oil and the building of the refinery attracted new people. From 1916 to 1969, the population of Curaçao increased fourfold; the greatest increase was from 1923 to 1948.

In recent years, while the overall population has been increasing, the number and percentage of foreigners in the population have been decreasing. For example, in 1959 there were 110,822 Netherlanders and 15,281 foreigners whereas in 1965 there were 125,580 Netherlanders and only 8,670 foreigners. Taking 1965 as the base, of the Netherlanders, 112,961 were Antilleans— 105,841 from Curaçao, 1,677 were born in Aruba, 3,643 in

Bonaire, and 1,800 in the Windward Islands. Of the non-Antillean Netherlanders, 6,585 were European born; 3,842 were Netherlanders born in foreign countries, many in Indonesia; and 2,202 from Surinam. Among the foreigners, there were 3,432 British, mostly West Indians; 1,882 Portuguese, mostly from Madiera; 1,183 Venezuelans; 412 Dominicans; 256 French, mostly West Indians; 207 United States citizens; 142 from Columbia; 158 Lebanese; and 72 Syrians. To emphasize further the diversity, the records show 79 different nationalities including (in addition to those mentioned above) Romanians, Germans, Turks, Cubans, East Indians, Costa Ricans, as well as one Ecuadorian and one Greek.

In terms of religious composition, in 1960 about 83 percent of the population was Catholic while about 10 percent was Protestant and less than one percent Jewish. In recent years many new Protestant groups have come to Curaçao and some of these, particularly the Seventh Day Adventists, have made a special effort to attract the nonwhite population.

The remnants of the previous stratification system are still evident. The bifurcated upper class is still composed of the descendants of the Sephardic Jews and of the Protestant Dutchmen. These Jews have been joined by Ashkenazian Jews (Eastern European) who came during the 1930s and 40s and who have moved also into retail trades. The Protestants also have been supplemented by other Dutchmen who came with the skills necessary for industrialization and others who were displaced from other former Dutch colonies that had gone the way of independence. Those from the newer groups cannot be considered upper class because they lacked the continuity to the past. They did, however, possess skills and resources that were necessary as Curaçao moved down the road to industrialization and many of them have prospered. There is still the small, heterogeneous middle class, generally characterized by lighter skin, more education, and better jobs, but their advancement has been somewhat impeded by the new layers of white migration from the outside. At the bottom is still the large black underclass, mostly Catholic. This category has become larger over the years primarily through natural increase rather than by further in-migration.

POLITICS AND GOVERNMENT

The establishment of the charter in 1954 was the culmination of changes that had been desired by many. Like all changes, the charter did not resolve issues in ways that pleased everyone. In addition, the charter set only the broad outlines of governmental structure, and within this structure political parties had to evolve that were both representative and effective.

One issue that continues to be problematic is the relation of Curaçao to the Netherlands. To many Antilleans, the semiindependent status of the country that was worked out in 1954 is still a satisfactory one. Many point out that it would be extremely costly for a country the size of the Netherlands Antilles to handle its own foreign affairs and national defense and that such a burden would even threaten its survival. Another argument used to support the existing relationship between the Antilles and the Netherlands is that it gives the former access to world trade markets that would otherwise be closed to it.

However sound such arguments seem to many, if not most Antilleans, they do not satisfy others who see in the limited autonomy of the country a continuation of its colonial status. The call for greater independence has come from such groups, particularly in recent times when nationalistic, anticolonial movements have emerged throughout the world, and when independence movements have even been successful in other areas of the Caribbean, such as in Jamaica and Trinidad. This pressure for change in the political status of the Antilles exerted by some groups in the society was one of the underlying strains that led to the May Movement. Some elements saw continued cultural as well as political domination by the Dutch in the kingdom government arrangement. To them, this meant that Antilleans would continue to measure themselves by Dutch values and would be destined to perceive themselves as failures. These elements suggested developing and accepting an Antillean culture and identity that would lead to self-respect, thus destroying the legacy of slavery and years of colonialism in the islands.

Interestingly enough, the question of independence from the

Dutch has been mirrored in debate over Papiamento, the native language. Dutch is the official language in the Antilles and is taught in the schools, reflecting the former colonial status of the Antilles and its present ties with the kingdom government. Many students in the Antilles enter school unfamiliar with Dutch because they come from backgrounds where Papiamento is spoken at home rather than Dutch. Such students—similar to blacks and other minorities in the Unites States who must learn English as spoken by the white middle class upon entering school—often experience considerable difficulty in learning Dutch. Some groups, including political and cultural nationalists, have advocated that Papiamento be declared the official language of the Antilles and that it be taught in the schools. The following passage from a report on the problems of economic development in Curaçao would seem to lend some support to those who call for such a change.

> It appears that there is a need to develop a uniquely Antillian educational system if economic development is to be realized. The costly statistic that 73 percent of the children repeat in the first six years of school argues strongly for change.[1]

Persons who have opposed such a move have employed arguments similar to those used against complete Antillean independence. For example, it is argued that Papiamento is an "underdeveloped" language and could not survive by itself. It is also suggested that it might not be worth the time and expense to develop the language into a flexible written form. Others who are opposed to the official recognition and use of Papiamento argue that, unlike Dutch, such a miniscule portion of the world speaks the language that it would lead to considerable difficulty and unnecessary expense when dealing with other nations.

Yet those who support the recognition of Papiamento as the official language of the country say such inconveniences, even if they were to occur, would be a small price to pay for the self-pride and confidence that the Antillean people would experience in using their own language. Such persons not only resent the fact that Dutch is the official language in the Antilles but also that many

Dutchmen while living in the Antilles never attempt to learn Papiamento.

In addition to the matter of the Antilles' relationship to Holland, the post-1954 period also saw the growth of discontent over local politics in Curaçao. One way to understand the politics of the Netherlands Antilles as it has developed is to see it as a continuing process of trying to set up coalition governments. Under the charter, the two major political blocs in Curaçao—the National People's Party (for years led by Moises Frumencio Da Costa Gómez) and the Democratic Party (founded by Efrain Jonckheer)—must depend on the votes of the people and parties of Aruba, Bonaire, and the Windward Islands in order to form a government for the Antilles. This requires a maximum of compromise and a minimum of ideology. The political parties are indigenous inventions. In 1936, discussion about independence and about the development of a meaningful franchise prompted the initial political parties. The parties, however, are tied up with particular people rather than specific issues, and are perhaps best described in these terms. Da Costa Gómez, a lawyer, started his political career as a member of the Roman Catholic Party, but finding the party too restrictive, he created the National People's Party (NVP) in the 1940s. Being "colored" himself (with a "Jewish" name) his party attracted primarily the black under class—urban laborers, rural workers, and farmers—which provided a large electoral base. The party also had some support from Catholics and Portuguese Jews. In the early 1950s, Da Costa Gómez headed a coalition government formed by his party and the AVP (Aruba People's Party). This NVP-AVP coalition also needed the added support of two smaller parties. Such a complex coalition was inherently weak and Da Costa Gómez dissolved it in 1954 when the charter went into effect and went back to the polls to get a stronger mandate.

In the 1940s the other major party, the Democratic Party (DP) was formed by Jonckheer, the great-grandson of a naval surgeon who arrived on the island in 1832. In the 1954 election, the

Democratic Party got the vote of the more urban and cosmopolitan sectors of Curaçao, including the support of many of the workers and union members. In turn, the opponents of the AVP on Aruba had formed a new party, Partido Patriótico Arubano (PPA). It also appealed to the urban and industrial workers. This DP-PPA coalition won ten seats in the Staten and needed two more to form the government. They were able to do this by gaining the support of the member from Bonaire and the member from the Windward Islands.

When the May Movement began in 1969, the Democratic Party had been in power since 1954. The party still led a coalition that controlled the Staten, and Ciro D. Kroon, leader of the DP, was prime minister. He had succeeded Jonckheer, the long-time party leader, as prime minister and party head. Jonckheer had become the minister at the Hague. Partly because it had fifteen years of uninterrupted power in the central government, the Democratic Party showed oligarchic tendencies, often refusing to cooperate with opposition parties and to consider needed reforms. However, its perpetual challenger, the National Party, could do little in the way of organizing an effective opposition at the central governmental level. The Democratic Party continued to draw its support from industrial groups and persons of Dutch and Protestant background as well as urban workers. Its connection with industrial interests and persons of Dutch ancestry had given it an establishment image in many quarters. And although there were some blacks in the party, it was severely criticized by some who believed that the black members were merely showpieces and that the party's main concern was to protect white interests. However, as is necessary for a successful party in Curaçao, it had also received much support from the urban working class. Kroon had been popular among workers because of his earlier connection with union organizing efforts. The party saw itself slightly left of center.

Ideologically, the National Party was very similar to the Democratic Party. Juan Evertsz became leader of the party after Da

Costa Gómez died in 1966. The party continued to draw its support from lower-class blacks in the rural area of Curaçao and lower middle-class groups in the urban area.

The two leading parties had both experienced serious internal problems prior to the May Movement. A power struggle had developed within the Democratic Party. Although Ciro Kroon had inherited the presidency of the party after serving it for many years, his leadership was challenged by a group of younger party members. The National Party was also the scene of a dispute just before the death of its founder, Da Costa Gómez. Some younger members had become dissatisfied with his leadership and the approach taken by the party and thus left it in 1965 to form a new party, the Union Reformista Antillano (URA). These internecine party struggles were a part of the ferment and change that emerged in Curaçao on the heels of the political reorganization of the Antilles in 1954.

POLITICS AND LABOR

Labor soon became a central element in Curaçao politics after the Antilles had achieved its autonomous status. Yet it is doubtful that this was realized by many persons in the union movement, especially those in the rank and file, prior to the emergence of the May Movement. The unions and workers were looked upon as an important source of support by those who wanted to maintain their positions of power, by those who wanted to acquire political power, and by those who sought social change. Some Democratic Party officials, including Kroon, had been involved in starting the labor movement in Curaçao. The party appealed to labor for its support and publicly expressed concern for the increasing unemployment and low wages in Curaçao. Because of their earlier connection with labor and their frequently declared support for its aims, the Democrats always had considerable support from labor in their reelection bids over the years. However, this also left a legacy of expectation among laborers that the Democratic Party would do something to alleviate the many economic problems that plagued them. The emergence of the May Movement was not unrelated to the fact that the Democratic Party, as the party in power in the central government, could not live up to such expectations. "Every time there was an election," observed one labor leader, "they would say, well, if we win you will get this and you will get that, but the labor leaders were not believing it anymore." Thus they began the May protest.

Political groups, such as the National Party and the recently formed URA Party, which sought to cut into the strength of the Democratic Party, also saw the labor movement as a potential power base. For example, when URA was formed it immediately sought labor support. A few labor leaders were even nominated for office by the party in order to attract the labor vote. Finally, groups that sought fundamental change in the Antilles also turned to labor for support. This was especially true of a group called the Vitó movement.

All of these competing groups courting the support of the working force helped to create conflict and competition between various segments of the labor movement as they responded to the appeals of different external groups. To some degree, the labor movement mirrored the various political tendencies in the society. Certain segments of the labor movement, either knowingly or unknowingly, supported the existing power arrangements in the society, others supported a transferal of power to other groups or parties, and a few even supported those who called for more fundamental social change.

PERSONAL POLITICS

Another important aspect of the contemporary political system is its particularistic nature. The personal appeal and style of politicians, for example, is often more important to voters than the ideological position they take or the party they belong to. Thus some political leaders like Ciro Kroon and Dr. Da Costa Gómez, who have been described as charismatic figures, were able to build large personal followings. Da Costa Gómez's personal appeal was so great that his widow was nominated for office by the National Party after his death in the hope that she could capture some of his former following. Curaçao, then, follows the Caribbean pattern of having charismatic-type leadership.[2] Charismatic leadership is important not only in political organizations in Curaçao but in other groups, such as labor unions, as well.

People in Curaçao also expect personal consideration and favors from politicians and government officials. "The political parties," observed one government official, "often have very personal relationships as the underlying relationships. You give favors to the one who votes for you, and you have to make sure you give them, and in exchange for that they vote for you." Citizens may even venture to the homes of politicians seeking personal favors and assistance. Labor also has a paternalistic orientation toward the government. During the May Movement workers expressed their puzzlement over the fact that the government had not tried to protect them from what they considered to be oppressive industrialists.

The stress on particularistic qualities is a general pattern in Curaçao and thus goes beyond the area of politics. This characteristic is probably related to some degree to the small size of the society. Many persons in Curaçao, including politicians and other leaders, use nicknames given to them by their families or friends with more frequency than their legal names. Such names function to personalize individuals.

In Curaçao, then, power and influence often hinged on personal appeal rather than universalistic considerations. As we shall see, this tendency was to play a significant role in the development of the May Movement and related events.

THE LABOR MOVEMENT

The labor movement in Curaçao should be viewed in the context of the economic situation of the society. Like other developing areas, Curaçao faces serious economic obstacles. Its economy has a very narrow resource base, for example. Phosphate is the island's major natural resource but it is increasingly becoming less economical to mine. The island is also handicapped by a small home market. On the other hand, Curaçao has an attractive climate, a beautiful city in Willemstad, and an excellent harbor. As a result, Curaçao's development has come to depend on tourism and trade with the outside world.

Another obstacle to economic development in Curaçao has been its heavy dependence on one industry, the oil industry, to supply jobs for its population. This industry, like many of those in other areas of the Caribbean, is experiencing a serious decline in the need for unskilled workers due to increasing mechanization. As a result of automation, the Royal Dutch Shell Company reduced its labor force from a peak of 11,000 in 1952 to about 4,000 in 1969. Initially this reduction affected only the imported workers—those from Portugal, Surinam, British and French West Indies, and Venezuela. By 1960, local workers were also being laid off. The employment decline, however, cannot be totally attributed to increased automation. Shell also decided to concentrate its efforts on refining. Many of the services that the company had previously provided, such as housing, and many of the subsidiary tasks, such as shipping and construction, were now subcontracted to other companies. At least part of the reason for this was to move away from the all-encompassing paternalism of the company. One consequence of this, however, was that there was often a major wage differential between Shell workers and employees of the newer companies working on Shell property. Sometimes a worker might find that his job was no longer with Shell and would be offered the same work with a new company at considerably less pay.

In the overall employment situation in Curaçao, the unemployment figure increased from 5,000 in 1961 to 8,000 in 1966.[3] Twenty percent of those seeking work in 1966 were unemployed.[4] These unfavorable changes in the economic picture in Curaçao have especially worked to the disadvantage of the unskilled work force. Table 1 shows the number and percentage unemployed in categories based on education. It indicates a somewhat dramatic and regular rise in the percentage unemployed as qualifications decline. Some labor leaders have blamed the unemployment among the unskilled, the bulk of whom are nonwhite, on the government's fiscal policies.

TABLE 1

NUMBER AND PERCENTAGE UNEMPLOYED
BASED ON EDUCATION AND VOCATIONAL TRAINING

| | MALE | | FEMALE | |
|---|---|---|---|---|
| | N | % | N | % |
| Less than 3 years of elementary school ........ | 1,572 | 31.1 | 584 | 18.9 |
| Three to 6 years of elementary school ........ | 2,311 | 45.7 | 1,434 | 46.5 |
| Advanced elementary school not completed .......... | 681 | 13.5 | 606 | 19.7 |
| Advanced elementary school completed ............. | 145 | 2.9 | 137 | 4.4 |
| Elementary vocational training ............... | 336 | 6.6 | 306 | 9.9 |
| Secondary school and higher education ......... | 11 | 0.2 | 14 | 0.5 |

SOURCE: *Netherlands Antilles 1969 Statistical Yearbook* (Willemstad: Bureau of Statistics, 1969), p. 61; "Curaçao: Economic Development" (Behavior Science Center, August, 1970), p. 4.

Attempts to encourage other types of economic enterprises to pick up the employment slack were restricted by the inherent limitations of the island's natural resources. The question of new directions for economic development was, of course, of critical concern to the government. The Democratic Party, the party in power, attempted to find economic alternatives and Kroon, who was economic minister during the 1960s, was centrally concerned with such planning. The alternatives that seemed realistically available to them centered on the development of the tourist trade, in building hotels, casinos, and the like, and also to a certain extent on industries that were dependent on raw materials that were inexpensive to import and required relatively unskilled labor. The government's economic policy was reflected in a 1965 report.

In order to prevent serious deterioration of the economy and living standard, all efforts must be directed to a further increase of domestic production outside the oil industry. . . . new private enterprises must be attracted in order to maintain the living standard. In 1953, a law for the "Promotion of Industrial Establishments and of Hotel Construction" was accepted by parliament. In this law, tax concessions are offered to new industries and hotels. From the beginning, it has been realized that additional concessions were necessary; in particular, for manufacturing industries, all of which have to import their raw materials.[5]

Although many new industries, such as hotels, attracted by the government's development incentives required high initial capital investments, they did not add impressively to opportunities for local employment, particularly the more highly paying jobs. An observation in an analysis of Curaçao's economy in the 1960s captures its character and problems.

> The economy is an agglomeration of foreign enclaves, a local oligarchy, a small middle class, workers, unemployed and the rural poor. While there have been and will continue to be odd points of growth—a new hotel perhaps—they affect little beyond immediate employment and purchases. There is little overall linkage. Most additional income goes into imports, to the upper classes and to foreign corporations. Areas in which local endeavors and investment can be productive remain hard to find or, when they appear, hard to grasp.[6]

The central government also pursued a policy of wage stabilization as part of its effort to attract new investors to the Antilles. This policy, which would later be modified somewhat as a result of the May Movement, affected government workers, many of whom at the lower levels were union members, as well as workers in commerce and industry. For example, in a previously cited document, the government boasted: "Wage stability has also been maintained by keeping government wages constant. The government wage has not been increased since 1958."[7] Some labor groups have been highly critical of the government's effort to stabilize wages and its policy of offering investment incentives to foreign companies, interpreting them as means of furthering the interests of Dutch and other capitalists to whom high government officials were said to be closely allied for reasons of class and race rather than as attempts to help unemployed workers who are mostly nonwhite. Since tourism has been one of the major industries the government has attempted to develop, some labor leaders have called to the attention of workers the difference between their standard of living as a result of low wages and unemployment and

TABLE 2

A SAMPLE OF WAGES IN THE NETHERLANDS ANTILLES
(IN ANTILLEAN GUILDERS: 1 NAf = U.S. $0.53)

|  | Minimum | Maximum |
|---|---|---|
| *Hourly* |  |  |
| Bus driver | 1.33 |  |
| Carpenter | 1.20 | 1.70 |
| Charwoman | .50 | .60 |
| Electrician | 1.20 | 1.90 |
| Female textile worker (Bonaire) | .50 |  |
| Foreman | 2.25 | 4.00 |
| Motor mechanic | 1.00 | 1.50 |
| Semiskilled laborer | 1.05 | 1.20 |
| Unskilled laborer | 1.00 | 1.10 |
| Welder | 1.20 | 2.10 |
| *Weekly* |  |  |
| Waiter | 40.00 | 80.00 |
| *Monthly* |  |  |
| Assistant accountant | 200.00 | 1,200.00 |
| Bookkeeper | 250.00 | 750.00 |
| Clerical worker | 250.00 | 750.00 |
| Domestic servants (live-in) | 60.00 | 70.00 |
| Typist | 160.00 | 225.00 |

SOURCE: *Investment Factors: Netherlands Antilles* (Willemstad: Department of Social and Economic Affairs, 1965), p. 32.

that of the increasingly visible and free-spending tourists who are mainly from the United States. This seems to have increased worker dissatisfaction in Curaçao. Wages in the Antilles are much lower than those in the United States. An idea of what wages were like in the mid-sixties in the Antilles can be seen in the sample of wages in several occupational categories shown in Table 2.

Let us now turn to the labor movement itself. The labor movement in Curaçao is fragmented and uneven. On the island there are large unions with well-trained leaders, but also many small ones with leaders who have received little formal training in union management. Furthermore, although unions within the same confederations have generally cooperated with one another, the overall pattern has been one of disunity, competition, and conflict. This pattern stems from a number of factors, the foremost being differences in ideology, international affiliation, local political allegiance, style and approach, and personal antagonisms between various union leaders.

As would be expected given its former colonial status, labor organization in the Netherlands served as the model for the labor movement in the Antilles. In the Netherlands there are three basic groups of trade unions: Protestant, Catholic, and Free, or Socialist. Roughly corresponding types can be found in the Antilles and are referred to as Independent, Catholic, and Free unions. The three groups of unions in the Netherlands often work with their counterparts in the Antilles, providing them with financial aid and advice. Prior to the May Movement, there was considerable conflict between the three groups of unions in Curaçao based in part on these varying international affiliations.

Of the three types of labor unions in Curaçao, the Free unions had the largest membership, were the best organized, and were the most influential. Several Free unions formed the largest confederation in Curaçao, the General Conference of Trade Unions (AVVC), which had a membership of around 12,000. One of the major unions affiliated with the AVVC was the Petroleum Workers Federation of Curaçao (PWFC), which had a membership of about 2,300. Because of its location at Shell, the heart of industry in Curaçao, the PWFC has played a major role in the labor movement. The labor agreements it has made with Shell, for example, have often become the standard used by other unions in their negotiations with management. Prior to the May Movement, relations with Shell were considered good by the leaders of the PWFC. As was generally true of other AVVC-affiliated unions, the leaders of the petroleum union took a gradualistic approach to negotiations and relations with management, and for this they were often criticized by the more radical unions and even sometimes by their own rank and file. One observer noted regarding the PWFC: "People thought that the union didn't act tough enough against Shell. The leaders of the union were always willing to see the other standpoint. That makes them reasonable people, but makes them in the eyes of the radicals actually not capable." The leaders of the petroleum union, as well as the leaders in other AVVC-linked unions, were generally sympathetic to the Democratic Party, the party in power in the central government. Thus they were criticized by the more radical unions of being allied with what the latter referred to as neo-colonial forces in Curaçao. However, in spite of this criticism, unlike trade unions in many developing societies, the Free unions in Curaçao did not directly become involved in politics or engage in "political unionism."[8] Indeed, most trade unions in Curaçao followed the pattern of the Free unions by not becoming directly involved in political activity. This was true even though a few labor leaders did run for political office.

The Curaçao Federation of Workers (CFW), a Free union affiliated with the AVVC, was to play an important role in the emergence of the May Movement. It is a general union representing workers from a wide variety of businesses and industries in Curaçao. Included in its membership are construction workers employed by the Werkspoor Caribbean Company, known locally as WESCAR, one of several companies under contract to do work for the Shell Company. As previously noted, it was a labor dispute between the CFW and WESCAR that led to the crisis that precipitated the May Movement.

In contrast to the tendency of most groups in the labor movement in Curaçao to be moderate and nonpolitical, as best exemplified by the Free unions we have mentioned, was a smaller number of groups with radical leaders. Such groups differed from the more moderate unions in that they: (1) had different international affiliations or allegiances, (2) had more militant and aggressive styles, and (3) saw the economic goals of the labor movement inexorably bound to political action.

Perhaps the most important radical union was the General Dock Workers Union (AHU), which was an Independent union led by two long-time labor leaders, Papa Godett and Amador Nita. This union espoused a revolutionary ideology and opposed the existing government and leading industrial groups on the grounds that they represented the colonial interests of Holland and erected barriers against the full participation of blacks in the economic and political life of the Antilles. Godett and Nita were given to flamboyant speech and their personal styles earned them considerable admiration among laborers, though the actual membership of their union was small. Both men were destined to play key roles in the May protest.

Other radical unions were found in the Catholic, or Christian, trade movement. This movement was founded in the late 1950s by a radical priest by the name of Father Amado Römer. Describing his philosophy as a "theology of revolution," Father Römer stressed the significance of the laborer's work in the society and the idea that it was their right to share in the rewards of the society rather than a privilege to be granted at will by some higher authority. The Curaçao Christian Confederation of Trade Unions (CCV) was the Catholic trade union's equivalent to the Free trade union movement's AVVC. The CCV was affiliated with the Latin American labor movement. Indicative of its political role, the CCV, under the direction of the CLASC movement,[9] had attempted to provide financial assistance for guerrillas working for the overthrow of the government in Haiti. Such direct political activity by the CCV created a great deal of concern among the more moderate unions in Curaçao who felt that the labor movement should focus exclusively on economic activity and not directly enter the political sphere. Leaders and supporters of the Christian trade movement in Curaçao were also involved in efforts to wrest power from the Democratic Party bloc by supporting URA, the leftist party that was formed by dissidents who left the National Party. Bèbè Rojer, the head of the CCV, became one of the party's candidates for public office.

Personal antagonisms between leaders in the various unions furthered the fragmentation within the labor movement. For example, some labor leaders competed to organize the same industry and such competition often took on the character of personal feuds. And because of Curaçao's small size, it was apparently more difficult to minimize personal hostilities through such normally effective techniques as avoidance.

In summary, prior to the May Movement, the labor movement in Curaçao was highly fragmented and largely nonpolitical, except for a small number of radical groups. However, part of the basis for more unified action existed in the strain many workers commonly felt, yet traditionally did not articulate, and the presence of charismatic figures in the dock workers union (and another radical group called Vitó, which we will discuss shortly) around whom workers could coalesce for political action.

### THE GROWTH OF RADICAL POLITICS

We have suggested that the reorganization of the Antillean government ushered in a period of change in the society. One change that was to have important consequences for the society was a new educational program that was established shortly after the new Antillean government came into being. Under this new government-sponsored program, scholarships were awarded to promising students for university study in the Netherlands. The person that was given much credit for this program was Dr. Da Costa Gómez who believed that students who benefited from the scholarships could return to the Antilles to assume positions of leadership. Many scholarship recipients did return to Curaçao to assume positions in the government and to teach school. However, others also became leaders in less traditional groups and organizations.

Some of the students who went to Holland on government scholarships were transformed in unanticipated ways. For many of the students, exposure to university life in Holland was a liberalizing, and even in some cases a radicalizing, experience. This made them less tolerant of the existing political and social arrangements in the Antilles. The first group of students began returning to Curaçao at the beginning of the 1960s. Out of this group came the nucleus for two leftist movements that were formed to challenge the established political and economic groups, such as the Democratic Party and the National Party, who were defined as self-serving and oligarchic.

Returning intellectuals helped form the Union Reformista Antillano (URA) in 1965. The impetus for the formation of this new party came from a dissident group within the National Party. The dissidents, led by Papy Jesurun, felt that the National Party had become conservative and ineffective. Much of the blame for the party's resistance to change and its inability to remain relevant was placed on its president, Dr. Da Costa Gómez. He was seen by the dissidents as an imposing charismatic figure who held tight control of the party and who steered it on a conservative course. The dissidents bolted the party and along with many young intellectuals who had recently returned from Holland formed URA with the aim of making it a progressive socialist party ideologically to the left of the two established parties.

Although declaring itself to the left of the other parties, URA, under the leadership of Jesurun, who became its president, was basically a reform movement rather than a revolutionary party. It appealed to labor for support and even placed a few labor leaders including Bèbè Rojer of the CCV on its list of candidates for public office. In 1967, the young party won two seats in the island legislature, and its leaders were confident that the party had a bright future in the political life of the country.

A radical movement that operated outside established politics was also organized by returning students and young intellectuals with the aim of disseminating ideas on the need for radical change in Curaçao. The movement published a paper for this purpose called *Vitó*, and the movement became known by that name. The paper took to task those forces in Curaçao identified responsible for the political and economic exploitation of the masses. Especially singled out was the Democratic Party and leading industries on the island. Such groups were viewed by the Vitó movement as allied with Dutch neo-colonial interests. Participants in the Vitó movement included schoolteachers and government workers. They were led by a young, white, former schoolteacher, Stanley Brown, who headed the volunteer staff that published *Vitó*. One observer noted regarding Brown:

> He writes stories that bring people to discredit and he is very specific. He is not always right in the way he states the facts but he doesn't care about it. He says for him it's the purpose that is to be reached that is important. You can't always use the proper methods.

This same person noted, ''This is a very Caribbean way of acting. Latin America has a long history of this sort of paper.''

Initially those in the Vitó movement were, as one of them put it, ''talking to themselves.'' The paper was written in Dutch rather than Papiamento and on a level that the intellectuals rather than the masses could understand and appreciate. Also, the young radicals had not become very involved in the more radical segments of the labor movement. However, this all changed in 1967. During that year, some of the core members of the Vitó movement decided that the only way in which significant change could be achieved in the society was for them to become directly involved in the labor movement. The paper began publishing in Papiamento to attract the attention of the masses, and special emphasis was given to radicalizing the labor unions.

*Vitó* became the chief communication link between the radical intellectuals and the labor movement. After it began publishing in Papiamento, several thousand copies were sold weekly. The staff conducted a systematic campaign to identify the political, social, and economic injustices that workers were said to experience in the society, with the aim of spurring them on to demand change. Published in the paper, for example, was information on the profits companies were said to be earning in order to dramatize the discrepancy between the condition of the workers and those of management. The radicals saw their role as that of a catalyst for social change.

The Vitó movement also attempted to influence the structure of the labor movement. As previously mentioned, the labor movement was highly fragmented as a result of such things as personal antagonisms and varying international affiliations. Vitó encouraged the labor unions to try and minimize their differences and work toward greater unification. For example, it tried to get the laborers to support one another (or at least not to fight openly) even though they had disagreements on the international level. Vitó also encouraged workers to bypass the leadership in their respective unions and develop unity and identification with fellow workers in other unions. The Vitó movement through its paper attacked those labor leaders and boards that were felt to hinder labor solidarity. This was done, for example, during union elections in an effort to influence their outcome.

Stanley Brown, the editor of *Vitó*, and Papa Godett, head of the dock workers union, became the key links between the radical intellectuals and the labor movement. This was very important in that they both had considerable influence within their respective constituencies. Brown was the most visible of the radical school-teachers and had a large following; Godett was admired by the rank and file throughout the labor movement. Brown and Godett worked together attempting to radicalize the labor movement; they supported the demands of workers for higher wages and aided them in their strike activity. Through the leadership of Brown, Vitó's involvement in the labor movement even included writing pamphlets for striking workers and contributing to strike funds.

Laborers in Curaçao were primarily concerned with wages. The young radicals in the Vitó movement sought to broaden the labor movement's interests to include political goals as well as bread-and-butter issues. For example, the Vitó movement tried to convince labor of the need for complete independence from the Netherlands. The movement also emphasized the need for Antilleans to become involved in a cultural revolution that would result in the widespread use and acceptance of Papiamento as their official language and the general recognition of an Antillean culture separate from the culture imposed upon them by the Dutch during the period of colonization. The young radicals also tied the political and economic plight of workers to their racial status, and exhorted them to demand the removal of all racial and class barriers to their effective participation in the society.

The young radicals in the Vitó movement were able to link their narrowly based group with the larger labor movement in Curaçao and sensitize some of the latter's members to the possibility of achieving broader goals. Many of the demands for change that were made during the May Movement can be partly attributed to this prior interaction between Vitó and the labor movement and the emergence of some common ideological ground. The prior relationship between Vitó and the general dock workers union especially was to play a significant role during the May Movement.

In summary, the period just prior to the May Movement was marked by considerable social change and strain in the Antilles, especially in Curaçao. The colonial status of the Antilles was modified in 1954 when it became a semi-independent part of the Netherlands, along with Surinam. Some Antilleans, however, were dissatisfied with the country's limited autonomy, viewing it as merely a continuation of their previous colonial status. Discontent over the long reign of the Democratic Party also developed. The party was seen in some circles as self-serving and incapable of solving the country's myriad economic problems. The labor movement in Curaçao also began its growth and development after semi-independence had been achieved. The highly fragmented labor movement perhaps felt the political, economic, and racial strains more than any other segment of the society. A new radical political movement called Vitó also emerged in the wake of the Antilles' new political status, largely owing its development to a university scholarship program sponsored by the reorganized central government. As we will presently show, the leaders of this movement and radical labor leaders with whom they had previously worked formed the nucleus of the May Movement and became a catalyst for social change.

On the eve of the May Movement then, there were many groups involved in the changing Curaçao scene. The key ones up to this point in our analysis are listed below. Of course, others will also be added to the list, many of whom grew directly out of the May Movement.

### Political Parties and Movements

Democratic Party of Curaçao (DP)
National People's Party of Curaçao (NVP)
Union Reformista Antillano (URA)
Vitó Movement

### Labor Unions

Free
General Conference of Trade Unions (AVVC)
Petroleum Workers Federation of Curaçao (PWFC)
Curaçao Federation of Workers (CFW)

Independent
General Dock Workers Union (AHU)
Catholic
Curaçao Christian Confederation of Trade Unions (CCV)


1. "Curaçao: Economic Development," report by Behavioral Science Center, August, 1970, p. 4. The report we have just cited is an economic analysis of Curaçao. Among the few sociological analyses are: A. F. Paula, *From Objective to Subjective Social Barriers* (Curaçao: De Curaçaosche Courant N.V., 1968); and R. A. Romer, *Ons Samenzijn in Sociologisch Perspectief: Ein Introductie in de Curacaose Samenleving* (Curaçao: G. C. T. vanDorp and Co., N.V., 1967). For a sociological study that compares various societies in the Caribbean including Curaçao see, H. Hoetink, *The Two Variants in Caribbean Race Relations* (London: Oxford University Press, 1967).

2. Harold Mitchell, *Contemporary Politics and Economics in the Caribbean* (Athens: Ohio University Press, 1968), p. 361.

3. *Netherlands Antilles 1969 Statistical Yearbook* (Willemstad: Bureau of Statistics, 1969), p. 61.

4. "Curaçao: Economic Development," p. 37.

5. *Investment Factors: Netherlands Antilles* (Willemstad: Department of Social and Economic Affairs, 1965), p. 23.

6. "Curaçao: Economic Development," p. 4.

7. *Investment Factors*, p. 24.

8. For a comprehensive discussion of political unionism in developing societies see, Bruce H. Millen, *The Political Role of Labor in Developing Countries* (Washington: The Brookings Institute, 1964). John Porter, see his *The Vertical Mosaic* (Toronto: University of Toronto Press, 1965), p. 314, notes that labor unions that engage in political activities can be viewed as social movements and those that don't as market unions. We take a similar position here. As increasing numbers of unions became political in Curaçao, the May Movement crystallized.

9. Paul E. Sigmund, ed., *The Ideologies of the Developing Nations* (New York: Praeger Publishers, 1967), p. 405.

# CHAPTER FOUR

# The Emergence of the May Movement

In the first chapter, we suggested that social movements develop within a particular sociohistorical context. That is to say, certain preconditions in a society set the stage for the appearance of social movements. Thus in Chapters two and three, we described the many historical and contemporary factors in Curaçao that we think were linked to the emergence of the May Movement in 1969. These factors included political, economic, and racial strains. We further suggested that such strains were exacerbated by the rapid change Curaçao and the rest of the Antilles were undergoing. This made Curaçao fertile ground for the emergence of a movement like the May Movement as well as for other changes. The analysis of preexisting conditions and change in Curaçao is not the sole object of this study, however. We are also interested in the career and internal dynamics of the May Movement and its consequences for the society. In this chapter, we will focus on the career of the May Movement and in the following chapter we will turn our attention to its impact on the island-society. Thus, from the standpoint of social change, we will have analyzed the May Movement in three ways: the role social change played in its formation, its internal changes, and the social change it in turn generated in the society.

The preexisting conditions in Curaçao that we have referred to were necessary rather than sufficient conditions for the emergence of the May Movement. Political, racial, and economic strains might have been present in the society for many years to come without spawning a movement like the May Movement. Often a major crisis will trigger the crystallization of an emerging social movement. In the case of the May Movement, a labor crisis transformed the fragmented labor movement in such a way as to enable it to engage in concerted action for the first time. During its career, the May Movement underwent both organizational and political changes. As we analyze the career of the May Movement, then, we will employ a political-organizational sequence model. This approach is similar to the natural-history approach in that it allows us to focus on the internal dynamics of the May Movement. However, it differs from natural-history models in that we do not imply that movements undergo an inevitable sequence of development. We suggest instead that the May Movement underwent certain changes rather than others because of the presence of particular internal and external factors.

LABOR UNREST

The Antilles were marked by substantial labor unrest in May of 1969. However, the major labor dispute and the one that eventually led to the mobilization of much of labor during the May Movement involved the Curaçao Federation of Labor (CFW), and WESCAR, one of several companies that did contract work for the Royal Dutch Shell Company. The dispute centered around two key issues. At WESCAR, non-Antillean workers—such as those from other Caribbean islands and Holland—were paid more than Antillean workers as compensation for working outside their own countries. Also, WESCAR employees received less pay than those at Shell for doing the same work. The WESCAR management claimed that being under contract to Shell it could not afford to pay its employees at the same rate as Shell employees. Thus the dispute between WESCAR and the CFW involved demands by the union that Antillean employees doing the same work receive pay equal to non-Antilleans, and that WESCAR employees engaged in the same work as those at Shell also receive equal pay.

During the month of May, the publishers of *Vitó* waged a strenuous campaign to keep the labor unrest at WESCAR and other companies in the Antilles, which they interpreted in leftist political terms, in the public limelight. News regarding strikes in various companies was featured in very dramatic terms. Also during the labor unrest, *Vitó* increased its attacks on the government and business groups for their "exploitation of the laboring class." The tone of the periodical's articles was particularly abrasive toward certain businesses and strongly hinted that action would or should be taken against them if conditions were not improved. One such article was in the form of an open letter to the owner of a large retail store, Tauber's, who had become the symbol of exploitative capitalism among radical union and intellectual groups. The letter was also addressed to "other capitalists of bad faith." In the letter, the owner of the retail store was asked if he had read the small print of his fire insurance policy, and if so, since the policy did not cover damages resulting from revolution and rebellion, it was difficult to understand why he followed a policy of exploitation in an age of Molotov cocktails and world-wide revolution by young people. (Interestingly enough, this man's store became a target of rioters on May 30, and was subsequently set afire and burned to the ground.) The headlines of another article that appeared in *Vitó* during this period read: "How Many More Days Before A Revolution?" The paper also featured stories about incidents involving workers that were interpreted as meaning that the laboring class was tired of being oppressed and was near revolution. Through its handling and interpretation of events during the May labor unrest, then, the Vitó movement escalated its efforts to provide cues for collective action for the labor movement at variance with the latter's traditional role.

EMERGENCE OF THE MAY MOVEMENT: ECONOMIC MOBILIZATION

A dramatic transformation of the labor movement in Curaçao began during this period of labor unrest in May, 1969. This transformation involved increasing solidarity within the labor movement[1] and increasing politicization. Factors both internal and external to the labor movement were responsible for these changes. During its transformation period, which we have labeled the May Movement, the labor movement went through four phases: an economic strike phase, a proto-political phase, a political strike phase, and finally a political party phase. The May Movement began with a very definite economic focus and gradually evolved into a mechanism for political as well as economic change. We will begin our discussion of the May Movement by considering its first phase, that is, the economic strike phase, and then proceed to discuss the more political phases in the order of their appearance.

*Economic Strike Phase*

The first phase of the May Movement involved an unusual show of solidarity by several unions in Curaçao. This solidarity came in the form of support given to the CFW, which went on strike against WESCAR for specific and limited economic objectives, and for this reason we have labeled this phase of the May Movement as the economic strike phase. During this initial phase, labor leaders mobilized workers around bread-and-butter issues. Since most unions in Curaçao did not traditionally become directly involved in politics and the fragmentation within the labor movement was due in part to the presence of groups and leaders with competing political styles and orientations, it seems highly unlikely that the May Movement could have initially crystallized around a political rather than an economic issue. On the other hand, a common position held even among the fragmented labor groups was that workers deserved higher wages. This common denominator, in contrast to the disagreement over the role of politics in reaching the goals of the labor movement, facilitated the emergence of support among labor groups for a sister union striking for higher wages.

The mobilization of the labor movement began on May 6, 1969, when some 400 WESCAR employees went on strike. This strike ended on May 8 with the two parties agreeing to negotiate for a new labor contract with the assistance of a government mediator. During the brief strike, Antillean workers were joined by non-Antillean workers at WESCAR. Also, the CFW received verbal and written support and encouragement from other unions in Curaçao.

Such expressions were forerunners of the increased solidarity to come. The negotiations between the CFW and WESCAR, which lasted for nearly three weeks, ended without a new agreement being concluded, and on May 27, the CFW went on strike a second time.

On May 28, during the lunch hour, a number of Shell employees and employees of other companies under contract to Shell demonstrated at Post V, the main gate of the Shell refinery, in support of the WESCAR strike. The next morning, May 29, about 800 persons working for contractors at Shell sites went on a peaceful sympathy strike at Post V. On the same day, the CFW received notice from the board of WESCAR that it considered the strike illegal and that all employees had to start back to work the next day or be discharged. That afternoon about 30 or 40 strikers, including several union leaders, marched to Fort Amsterdam, the seat of the Antillean government. They held a demonstration, and their spokesmen were heard by a mediator from the Social and Economic Affairs Department. One of the concerns of the strikers was that the government itself was interested in keeping wages low in order to attract foreign investors. Such issues were to become more salient in the political phases of the May Movement.

At 7:30 P.M. on May 29, a meeting was held by the PWFC at Casa Sindical, the headquarters and meeting place for several of the Free labor unions. Also in attendance at this meeting were strikers from WESCAR. The meeting was called to determine the position the PWFC would assume in the labor crisis. The PWFC had never in the past made common cause with the employees of companies doing work under contract for Shell, which the CFW represented. However, the position that the PWFC took in the labor dispute would be crucial in that it was the largest union in the oil industry in Curaçao, and its labor contract with Shell, which made its members the highest paid workers in the industry, served as the basis for the aspirations of the strikers.

The leaders of the PWFC came under considerable pressure to show their solidarity with the growing strike movement by calling a strike of Shell. This pressure emanated from several sources. First, by the time of this meeting several other groups of workers had united behind the strikers either by going out on strike themselves or by giving support to them in public announcements and in statements issued to government officials. For example, the latter was done by the large General Conference of Trade Unions (AVVC) to which the PWFC was affiliated. Also, the radical segment of labor exerted pressure upon the PWFC to show solidarity with the strikers. Finally, there was strong sentiment among the rank and file of the PWFC to support the other strikers by going out on strike against Shell. This sympathy of the rank and file for the cause of the CFW strikers can be traced in part to the efforts of radicals like Godett and Brown who went among the workers during the crisis calling for united action against their common foe, the business community. Given these pressures, the leaders of the PWFC felt that they had no choice but to call for a strike. They believed that to do otherwise would cost them the control of the union. Significantly then the moderate leaders of the all important petroleum workers union who generally preferred negotiation and accommodation to more militant tactics were effectively neutralized at least in part by the actions of more radical labor leaders. Thus at the meeting, it was decided to call a 24-hour sympathy strike of all Shell employees. The decision to strike was made at about 8:30 P.M. and was to take effect at 11:30 that same evening. After the meeting, a large portion of the gathering, estimated to be around 1,000, left by cars for the various gates of the Shell refinery to inform workers who would be reporting to work on late shifts about the union's decision to strike. Many of the workers on the job at Shell left immediately upon hearing the decision to strike. Shell began to call in supervisory personnel to take over operations and some of them were harassed by strikers at the gates.

Although a portion of the gathering from the union meeting had gone to the Shell gates, the number of persons in front of the union hall increased, and the crowd started harassing passers by and stopping cars. Particular attention seemed to be given to cars that contained or were suspected of containing "European Dutchmen" or Makamba (i.e., Dutchmen who had recently come from Holland in contrast to persons of Dutch ancestry born in the Antilles).

Around midnight, about 1,000 men were gathered at Post V. There harassment of supervisory Shell personnel occurred, especially European Dutchmen, and some temporary road barriers were destroyed. The crowd, however, began to dissolve about 2:30 A.M., and the rest of the night was relatively quiet. Yet the conflict that occurred at the entrance to the Shell refinery, and that which had occurred earlier in front of the union headquarters, were forerunners of things to come in the second phase of the May Movement.

The first phase of the May Movement, then, involved primarily strike activity on the part of workers directed at economic conditions. Other kinds of strains were also reflected in the early actions of some of the workers, however. For example, racial and political discontent was expressed by the occasional harassment of whites identified as European Dutchmen, and claims made that the government might be directly responsible for the crisis by pursuing the policy of encouraging industry to keep salaries low. Nevertheless, for most of the workers the expression of political or racial discontent did not occur until sometime later.

### ELABORATION OF THE MAY MOVEMENT: POLITICIZATION

On the morning of May 30, more unions announced that they had gone on strike in support of the CFW. Starting around 7:00 A.M. the number of strikers and other persons at Post V grew rapidly, and by 7:30 it was estimated that between three and four thousand men had gathered there. Union leaders began making speeches to the gathering. The head of the CFW appealed to the strikers to keep politics out of the protest. However, Papa Godett, the head of the radical dock workers union, began moving the issue in the direction of politics by criticizing the actions of the government during the crisis and calling for the strikers to march to Fort Amsterdam to overthrow it.

Up until the point when Papa Godett sounded the keynote for political action, the May Movement had essentially an economic orientation. At least this was the orientation preferred by the more moderate leaders in such unions as the CFW and the PWFC. However, certain factors, both background and immediate, converged making the politicization of the movement highly probable. The first has to do with the nature of the social structure of underdeveloped societies like Curaçao. Since economic development is so important as well as precarious in underdeveloped societies, the government rather than business often establishes policies of direct concern to labor unions such as wages, hours, and employment practices. As a result, in many underdeveloped societies, labor unions have to directly enter the political arena, that is, engage in political unionism, if they are to make changes in their economic situation. Sufrin has noted for example, "In well developed economies, trade unions adjust and adapt to industrial and governmental organization. The same is true for developing societies, but the more significant type of adjustment and adaptation in the latter is to government because it is the more significant institution from the viewpoint of the interests of the trade unions."[2] The Antillean government had assumed a role that was somewhat typical in a developing society. For example, it pursued a policy of encouraging industries to stabilize wages in order to attract new investors. In such a context, when economic institutions or arrangements are not clearly differentiated from political ones, economic issues become political ones as well, and an initial economic-social movement may evolve into a political movement. Thus Curaçao was structurally conducive to the emergence of political as well as economic protest activity by labor unions.[3] The presence of leaders who could articulate political aspirations for the labor movement and had broad appeal among workers also facilitated the shift of the May protest from a primarily economic to a political character. For example, prior to the labor crisis, radical leaders like Papa Godett and Stanley Brown of the Vitó movement had established themselves among workers in Curaçao as important leaders who were prepared to lead them into political action. Yet the two variables mentioned thus far were only necessary and not sufficient conditions in the politicization of the May Movement because they had been present in the society for a long time without generating significant political action on the part of labor. The final ingredient in the equation that led to the politicization of labor appears to have been its initial economic mobilization that brought together large numbers of workers. Once mobilized, the labor movement began to perceive a political role for itself that was generally unrecognized prior to the crisis. As long as labor was composed of isolated and competing factions, even with the existence of the background variables mentioned above, it did not engage in direct political activity. However, as a result of the sense of solidarity and power felt once they were mobilized at the beginning of the May Movement, the workers were encouraged to engage in collective political activity. This activity was fairly unstructured initially, but assumed a more organized character later. And as was the case in its confrontation with the business groups, the polarization between the labor movement and political authorities furthered the growth of solidarity within the former.

Finally, once the political protest activity of the May Movement was started, it was furthered at certain points by the actions of external groups. For example, in some cases this involved receiving support from similarly dissatisfied groups, and, in others, this entailed the nature of the response of social control authorities. We will now turn to a discussion of those phases of the May Movement whose objectives became increasingly political in nature.

### Proto-Political Phase

The strike began to assume political significance as Papa Godett and other labor leaders called for a march on the government at Fort Amsterdam about seven miles away in downtown Willemstad. The gathering had grown to about 5,000 as it moved out toward the center of Willemstad led by Papa Godett and several other labor leaders in a jeep. However, the political objective of forcing the government to resign was never to be achieved by this particular group as it was later to break up and engage in generally uncoordinated protest characteristic of proto-political social movements, that is, movements that represent an early or initial form of political action.

Proto-political movements, or what some scholars have referred to as anomic movements,[4] occur among groups in a society that feel that the more traditional means for bringing about change are either closed to them or are no longer effective.[5] Segments of the labor movement in Curaçao were dissatisfied with the response of the government to the plight of workers and were also discouraged by the prospect for changing the government's approach to the problem. It was within this context that the proto-political phase of the May protest emerged.

Willemstad is located on the southern shore of the island of Curaçao. A picturesque canal-like inlet called Saint Anna's Bay bisects the city, dividing it into the sections known as the Punda and Otrabanda. Curaçao's famed pontoon bridge connects the two areas. The bridge opens about twenty times a day to let ships enter and leave. Saint Anna's Bay is the route of access to a larger bay called Schottegat. The Shell refinery is located on the farther side of Schottegat, almost directly opposite the inlet separating the two parts of the city. Willemstad can be reached from Post V then by way of the Punda or Otrabanda. Although they are nearly equidistant, the route to the Punda is a better access route through the built-up portions of the periphery of the city. Fort Amsterdam is also located on the Punda side. The marchers took the approximately seven-mile route by way of the Punda.

The leaders of the march had not made plans to control the huge gathering. For example, crowd marshals were not appointed. One leader explained this later by saying that no difficulty was anticipated and so no such precautions seemed warranted. The leaders of the march had no control, of course, over who joined the protest. Thus in addition to the group of strikers and onlookers that had initially assembled at Post V, many persons along the route of march to Willemstad joined the ranks of the protestors, most noticeably young males. One of the strike leaders indicated that he began noticing youths joining the march after it had progressed about a mile and a half in the direction of Willemstad.

As the crowd moved toward downtown Willemstad, ostensibly to register its protest with the government, it shifted between acts of harassment to violence of a more dramatic and serious nature. Cars coming the other way were pushed aside and some were turned over. A pickup truck driven by a white man was set on fire. A large supermarket was looted, as was a white-owned fruitstore-carryout. At both stores, a large quantity of liquor was taken and consumed by some of the marchers along the way. (It had been reported earlier that many of the persons at Post V during the night had been drinking.) Many youths began joining the march. A large bus was stopped on a major traffic circle and its windows were shattered. With this initial damage, word soon reached the city of the potential danger, and most traffic was forewarned to avoid the route the marchers had taken. The chief of police also warned merchants in the city to close their shops for the time being. This later resulted in many stores being easy prey for looters as many merchants interpreted the police chief to mean that they and their employees should leave the stores.

As the marchers moved down the road, the windows in several large commercial buildings were smashed, including those of an electrical and air-conditioning contractor and a Coca-Cola bottling plant. More cars were damaged and set on fire. As would be the case when the riot reached its peak as the protestors arrived in the heart of Willemstad, during this period some of the targets, according to some protestors, were deliberately chosen because of past grievances. For example, the windows in Texas Instruments, an American-owned company, were broken and some of the marchers went inside and threatened the workers. The company stopped production as a result of this. The company had earned the reputation of being exploitative because it had resisted efforts by workers at unionization. Also during this period as well as later, while some targets might have been deliberately selected, other potential ones were ignored by the protestors. Residences were spared, although the inhabitants of some homes were forced to leave them because of smoke from fires set in commercial buildings. Also public and quasi-public buildings were spared by the protestors throughout the riot, even as nearby commercial properties were attacked.

The small Curaçao police force was mobilized when it received intelligence reports on the increasingly violent march. Also, before noon the assistance of the local militia, called the voluntary corps, and the Dutch Marines stationed in Curaçao was requested. A police unit was sent to intercept the marchers before they reached downtown Willemstad. The police were given orders to first be firm with the protestors and if that didn't work to shoot over their heads, and, if that also failed to control them, as a last resort, to shoot in the legs those who didn't respond to their authority. The police were unsuccessful in their first attempt to halt the march. They soon became surrounded by the protestors, who attempted to run them down with some of the cars that were in the march. It appears that the inability of the under-manned police to enforce their authority facilitated the escalation of the violence.[6] The police set up a second line of defense at Berg Altena, a hill that overlooks the downtown area. At this point there were about sixty policemen present. The police officer in charge talked to the leaders of the march. About this time Papa Godett was shot in the back when according to some observers he was attempting to talk to the crowd. Godett later claimed that he believed he was shot because the government had given orders to kill him. The police reported that they were being heavily stoned and threatened by the marchers at the time Godett was shot. One high police official said of the situation his men were in, "They had to fight for their lives." This incident marked a significant turning point in the disturbance. The confrontation between the marchers and the police escalated, soon to be followed by the major looting and arson that would not abate until increased force was applied. A car was overturned and burned on the hill. One of two fire trucks that had been sent to support the police was set on fire and pushed in the direction of the police lines. The man at the steering wheel, later identified as an employee of WESCAR, was shot and killed. As the pitched battle continued, the police suffered injuries from thrown rocks, and three police cars and another fire truck were damaged. A Red Cross ambulance sent into the area was also stoned.

When the union leader was shot, he was taken immediately to the hospital by other union leaders who had been with him. Some of the marchers also followed to the hospital. During the next several hours, it was rumored that Godett was dead. Because of the nature of his injury, he had to spend considerable time in the operating room. Afterwards, several of the union leaders were permitted to see him to assure them that he was alive. The scene at the hospital was characterized by a great deal of bedlam when the labor leaders brought Godett in and at other times during the disturbance. One observer remarked in reference to the crowded and confused conditions as the injured were brought in and relatives arrived, ''It was horrible. It was a revolution at the hospital.'' The types of injuries suffered by the wounded brought to the hospital included burns, bullet wounds, and cuts.

With the shooting of Godett and the absence of the other leaders who accompanied him to the hospital, the bulk of the crowd quickly moved into Willemstad's business district on the Punda side of Saint Anna's Bay, spreading out through the streets, breaking windows, and looting. The crowd broke up into smaller groups, in many cases into groups of three and four persons, and moved along the narrow streets where retail stores were located. Eyewitnesses consistently reported that most of the rioters were young men in their teens and early twenties and that few women were involved. The latter was reflected in the fact that very few women were arrested during the disorders.

Although some rioters stayed on the Punda side of the business district, others moved across the pontoon bridge, which spans the bay, to the Otrabanda area and looted shops. Fires were set in both the Punda and Otrabanda areas. The police made arrests. Significantly, at noon the first fire on the Otrabanda side was set at Tauber's, the retail store that had been earlier singled out by the radical paper *Vitó* as being a particularly exploitative business establishment. The fire soon spread to other buildings in the area.

At one point, the fire at Tauber's was brought under control; however, after the police who had been guarding it left, arsonists returned and reset the fire and the building burned down. An old theatre that was used for storing goods, including considerable quantities of liquor, was looted and burned. Back across the bay, a number of fires were set in stores that had already been looted. Some of the buildings that housed the shops were several hundred years old and burned rapidly as the fires spread from roof to roof. The compactness of the business district made access difficult for fire-fighting equipment. Also fire fighters were hampered by the fact that some equipment had been destroyed earlier in the day. Boats were used to fight fires in buildings near the waterfront.

The policemen, who also double as firemen in Curaçao, were joined by several organizations and private citizens in performing emergency roles during the disturbance. The detachment of marines stationed in Curaçao, as well as marines later flown in from the Netherlands, worked under the authority of the local police. The marines assisted in fighting fires, engaged in crowd control activities, and patrolled the downtown business areas, and also guarded strategic structures such as the pontoon bridge. There had been attempts by rioters to damage the bridge, which if successful would have made it more difficult for fire-fighting equipment to reach the Otrabanda. The voluntary corps worked in cooperation with the police and marines in fighting fires, patrolling the riot-torn area, and guarding banks, radio stations, and other key enterprises. According to reports by members of the voluntary corps and other observers, the voluntary corps had less difficulty with protestors than the police or marines. For example, the voluntary corps did not experience the verbal abuse from protestors that the marines took even as late as June 1. Those in the voluntary corps felt that they were accepted more than the police or marines because they were volunteers. The Red Cross and the Rescue Squad, another volunteer group, also were mobilized. The Rescue Squad worked in the riot-torn area picking up the wounded, later treating many of them at Squad headquarters. The Squad also set up a first-aid station and worked at the hospital. The

Red Cross also established an aid station and treated the wounded. Private citizens assisted many groups in fighting fires and other emergency work. In some cases this was on a long-term basis while in others it was of brief, on-the-spot duration. In one case of the latter variety, for example, a high government official with the aid of passers-by was able to remove a burning drum filled with highly combustible material that had been placed against a bank, thus preventing damage to the building.

In the afternoon of May 30, several clergymen in Curaçao made an appeal over the radio for an end to the violence that had erupted. One noted, ''Punda is on fire. Curaçao is in a state of alarm due to the activities of the striking employees. I appeal to the workers who are fighting for just pay to stop their activities. I hope that from the remaining ruins a new and better Curaçao will rise.''[7]

Emergency organizations continued fighting fires during the night of May 30 and the next day before they were brought under control. A curfew was enforced from the evening of May 30 to June 2. The downtown riot area was closed off to unauthorized persons and a ban on assembly was imposed as well as on the sale of liquor.

A leaflet distributed in Curaçao on May 31, which was attributed to the Vitó movement, read in part:

> The people, especially the workers, who have already suffered for many years and have endured many situations have become fed up with it all!
> The people have become fed up!
> The workers have become fed up!
> Willemstad has burned!
> For the first time in history, the people have reacted and behaved in a manner which was thought impossible.
> Willemstad has burned!
> The people could loot and get away with it.
> The people have already showed that they are fed up.
> This is the lesson for the exploiters. . . .
> Now that we have burned everything down, there is new room to start building again. Now we must plant something new, and the entire population is requested to help. . . .
> The exploiters have been taught a lesson.

The authorities, who have always thwarted the people, have been taught a lesson.
Willemstad has burned, and we will have to rebuild it.[8]

On May 31, the day after the major disorders started, the violence began tapering off. From this point on, authorities were mainly concerned with controlling the ''hit and run tactics of youths.'' No significant outbreaks of violence occurred between May 31 and June 1. On June 1, exhausted local security forces were supplemented by 300 marines flown from the Netherlands.

For a short period, the protest in Curaçao even spilled outside the island. Some 300 to 500 persons, including Antillean students and workers and Dutch students and radicals, held a protest demonstration at the Hague in Holland on June 1, after learning about the developments in Curaçao. The demonstrators, marching in support of the workers and unions in Curaçao, protested the use of Dutch Marines there and called for Antillean independence from Holland. Carrying posters with such slogans written on them as: ''Invasion Troops Out,'' ''No Troops, But Work,'' ''Colonial Murder,'' and ''Slaves Fight for Freedom,'' the protestors sent a delegation to meet with Dutch government officials to deliver a letter of protest. There were also clashes and fights between some of the demonstrators and the police. The protest lasted for a few

TABLE 3

COSTS OF THE MAY VIOLENCE

| *Personal* | |
|---|---|
| Deaths | 2 |
| Injured (excluding those slightly injured) | |
| Police officers | 22 |
| Others | 57 |
| Arrests | |
| Men | 308 |
| Women | 14 |
| *Property* | |
| Businesses burned out | 43 |
| Other buildings burned | 10 |
| Damaged and looted | 100 |
| Damaged only | 90 |
| Vehicles destroyed by fire | 30 |

SOURCE: Compiled from various reports and interviews.

hours and by the time it had ended several of the participants had been arrested by the police.

In the weeks after the violence in Curaçao, there was an accounting of its social and economic costs. They were as reported in table 3. Estimates of the dollar damage ranged from 35 to 40 million dollars.

On June 2, the following commentary appeared in a local Curaçao paper which suggested that while peace was being restored to the island, other crises and changes were still to come.

> After the horrible events of last Friday it seems that peace has returned to Curaçao. There weren't any serious incidents on Saturday and Sunday. This morning it was enormously crowded in the city center, especially on the Punda side. The almost unimaginable event occurred this morning at about nine o'clock when several hundred people gathered in front of La Bohemia shop . . . and stole many shop goods. According to bystanders the owner of the shop would have given the people permission to take the goods. If this is true, which we haven't been able to verify with the owner, this would be an outrageous situation in view of the past events. Only about 45 minutes later policemen and marines arrived on the scene to chase the people away. A strange and unimaginable affair. At the moment many foreign journalists from many countries, especially from the Netherlands, America and Venezuela, are staying in Curaçao, indicating that what has occurred here recently is regarded as world news. Everywhere now responsible people urge others to stay calm and keep the peace. . . .
>
> At the moment many rumors are circulating such as the one that they are missing explosives at the Curaçao Mining Company which could be used for destructive purposes. . . . There exists great danger in such rumors and accusations. . . .
>
> In the waters surrounding Curaçao, two American war ships have been seen. We could not get any official information about their presence. We also have tried to get some information about the meeting and discussions which were held between the union leaders and the members of the Staten, however this was impossible. We wait in suspense to get the results of the meeting of the Staten which will be held this afternoon. We hope that everybody will keep cool and that attention will be paid only to the interest of the society and the measures to be taken in order to reconstruct Curaçao.[9]

At 4:30 P.M. on May 30, the head of the CFW announced by radio that the union had reached a one-year agreement with WESCAR and that the principle of equal wages for equal work on Shell sites had been accepted. He also announced that the strike at Shell by the PWFC was ended. Thus the agreement with WESCAR meant that the initial economic goal of the May Movement had been achieved. However, this did not mean that the end of the movement had been reached because the second phase, that is, the proto-political phase, had signaled political as well as economic discontent on the part of the workers in Curaçao.

Such outbursts as the one that occurred in Curaçao can be viewed as a primitive, or rudimentary, form of political activity. By themselves, because the demands they articulate are vague and concerted action limited, they do not directly achieve long-range goals. However, unplanned outbursts may evolve into more organized protest thus developing the capacity for recalling a government and making other changes.[10] Thus in Curaçao several unions recognizing the political significance and potential of the outburst formed a coalition to state in specific terms that which was expressed in vague terms by the rioters, that is, the need for political change. At this point, the May Movement entered a third phase—a political strike phase.

*Political Strike Phase*

During the height of the outburst on May 30, unsuccessful attempts were made by some moderate labor leaders who had not been in the march to arrange a meeting with the government to discuss the growing crisis. Finally, a meeting was held by labor leaders from several of the unions in Curaçao, both moderate and radical, during which it was decided to send an ultimatum to the government calling for its resignation and new elections, otherwise a general strike would be declared.[11] This ultimatum was signed by the union leaders and sent by messenger to the government around 8:00 P.M. About 9:00 P.M. the unions' ultimatum was also delivered over the radio by the head of the CFW and Amador

Nita, the secretary-general of the dock workers union. This later resulted in the latter's arrest, but pressure from the unions led to his subsequent release. In accounting for their unprecedented actions, the unions declared that they were convinced that the government's social and economic policies had failed and that the rights of the workers had not advanced along with the development of the country. As a result, they reasoned, the workers had become frustrated and this frustration resulted in the outburst. Thus the growing belief among the labor unions was that significant change could occur only through political action. This emerging ideology clearly marked a break from the traditional stance taken by most trade unions in Curaçao.

At 2:00 P.M. on May 31, the unions held another meeting and this time representatives from several unions from Aruba, the second most populous island in the Antilles, were in attendance. Also present were representatives from the chamber of commerce. The latter were invited to the meeting to essentially serve as the channel of communication between the unions and the government. The utilization of such a go-between further demonstrated the isolation the unions felt from the government.

At this important meeting, the Aruban unions indicated their support of the call for the government's resignation, which had been made the day before. A joint statement was issued by the two groups of unions declaring that a general strike would be called in both Curaçao and Aruba if the government did not agree to step down within forty-eight hours. Thus with this joint action, the boundaries of the May Movement were extended beyond Curaçao and at the same time its power was enhanced. Finally, the union leaders explained to the chamber of commerce representatives why a general strike was going to be called so that they could relay the mood and position of the unions to government officials. The chamber of commerce representatives agreed to talk to the government to determine if it would resign as demanded by the coalition of unions or make other concessions that might end the crisis.

On June 1, the unions again met with the chamber of commerce representatives who brought the government's reply that it was willing to talk only after there was complete order in Curaçao, and before that it would do nothing. The next action taken by the union coalition was to request that they be allowed to come before the Staten, which was to meet the following day, June 2. That night the unions received word from the president of the Staten that their request was approved and so they decided to postpone the general strike until they saw what the consequences of their meeting with the Staten would be. The next day the unions met with the Staten and reiterated their lack of confidence in the government and again called for its resignation. On the following day, June 3, the Staten voted to dissolve the government and to set new elections for September 5, 1969. Thereafter the prime minister resigned and an interim government was set up with a new prime minister to carry out routine governmental activities and to arrange for the September elections. Thus there was no need for the unions to put into effect the general strike plans they had drawn up during their several days of meetings, which included the disruption of such essentials as electricity and water services.

In sum, the political or general strike phase, which grew out of the proto-political phase of the May Movement, marked the first time in the Antilles that a coalition had been formed by the various segments of labor who were more accustomed to conflict and competition than cooperation. In the political strike phase, the unions organized the protest of the rioters and articulated it in specific political terms that led to the recall of the government. However, this third phase of the May Movement was to give way to another, the political party phase.

*Political Party Phase*

Even more structure and conscious emphasis upon long-range political goals developed in the May Movement when it served as the basis for the formation of a new labor party. With the formation of the party, a political ideology had to be formulated, candidates selected, and a campaign organized. As has often been true in other developing societies, those persons whose experiences had provided them with considerable political concern joined in the effort to make the May Movement a truly organized political form. This included radical union leaders as well as intellectuals in the Vitó movement who had returned to Curaçao after studying in Dutch universities. As Oppenheimer has noted, the latter have historically played leading roles in the transformation of movements from proto-political to organized political enterprises such as independence movements.[12]

The new political party, called the May 30 Labor and Liberation Front, was formed in June. Forming the cadre of this political party were three men who had played key roles in earlier phases of the May Movement: Papa Godett and Amador Nita of the dock workers union, and Stanley Brown, publisher of the radical *Vitó* paper. These men had a large following among the laborers in Curaçao before the May Movement, and their actions during it only served to enhance their appeal. All three men had been arrested as a result of their activity during the crisis, and Brown, who was sentenced to jail for a term of several months on a charge of agitation, was in confinement during the party's election campaign. In addition to being arrested like the other two leaders, Godett was wounded during the outburst on May 30. These three men had high visibility, then, and became symbols of the May protest.

Elections involve considerable fanfare in Curaçao with candidates making many public speeches and parties using the mass media to get their campaign messages and slogans to the public. Much use is also made by competing parties of such election paraphernalia as campaign buttons, banners, and posters. The special September 5 election was no exception to this pattern. There were four opposing Curaçao parties in the election: the Democratic Party, the National People's Party, URA, and the Liberation Front. In Antillean elections, each party places at the head of its list of candidates the person it considers to have the most personal appeal and to be its top vote getter. Former prime minister

Kroon headed the Democrats' slate of candidates, Juan Evertsz headed the National Party's list, Papy Jesurun carried the banner for URA, and Papa Godett, because of his likely appeal to workers as a result of his role in the May protest, headed the list for the Liberation Front, which also included Nita and Brown. One party spokesman, for example, declared that Godett was chosen to lead the party in the campaign because he was "the person to receive the first bullet" during the rebellion. Even though he was prime minister and leader of the ruling Democratic Party at the time of the May rebellion, Kroon accepted none of the responsibility for it. He campaigned for law and order, suggesting that his party could provide it for the Antilles in contrast to those who would bring on more insurrection and instability. The National Party and URA offered little in the way of new programs in their campaigns. They were to later accuse the Liberation Front of cutting into their strength by taking a "racial approach." Some members of URA left the party during the campaign to join the Liberation Front's effort when it became clear to them that the approach URA was taking would basically be no more progressive than that of the Democrats and Nationalists.

During its campaign, the Liberation Front held public rallies around the island. Dressed in military fatigues and using such props as a campaign poster depicting former prime minister Kroon shooting May protestors, the party's message delivered by the candidates was similar to the one that had been stated in more vague terms by the rioters. It was anti-Dutch, emphasized the need for black pride and a positive Antillean identity, and called for the establishment of a government that would be responsive to the needs of the laboring class rather than to a business and neo-colonial elite. It called on the workers to turn away from the established parties and join in the effort to develop a mass-based labor party.

Stanley Brown had a significant impact on the Liberation Front's campaign even though he was imprisoned at the time. Due in large measure to his identification with the party, the Liberation Front received the backing of many radical teachers and intellectuals. Some made speeches on behalf of the party during the campaign as well as financial contributions. The Liberation Front also benefitted from support that came from the dissident group that broke away from URA because it felt the party was pursuing policies that were too moderate after beginning as a radical alternative to the Democratic and National parties. Additionally, efforts were made to organize support for the Liberation Front by some persons not because they favored its politics but because they saw an opportunity to end the fifteen-year reign of the Democrats and thereby create a fluid political situation that they might later be able to use to their own advantage. Such was the case, for example, with one prominent Curaçaon who made considerable effort to gather voter support for the Liberation Front because he had ambitions for establishing his own political party and believed that he would be most successful in doing this with a weakened Democratic Party. As he later put it himself, he "needed someone to break their backs." He suggested that he was in a position to organize three to four thousand votes for the Liberation Front. All this external support for the new labor party facilitated the continued development of the May Movement in a political direction.

For a new party, the Liberation Front achieved unusual success when the elections were held on September 5. It managed to win 3 of the 22 seats in the Staten and Godett, Nita, and Brown occupied these seats and continued to serve as visible symbols of the May Movement by their unorthodox styles and rhetoric. It also turned out that the cooperation of the new party was needed to form a new coalition government and as a result the Liberation Front was given two ministerial posts.

The formation of the political party was an attempt to routinize the growing sentiment among the ranks of labor during the crisis that significant changes could be realized only to the extent that it directly entered the political arena. Overall, this development follows the pattern of most developing nations, with the possible exception that in Curaçao it occurred in a very short time span.

Without subscribing to a rigid natural-history approach, this analysis offers evidence of the tendency of prepolitical and proto-political movements to be replaced by more organized political forms providing that certain facilitating conditions exist. If the necessary facilitating conditions had not been present, the May protest in Curaçao could have conceivably assumed a nonpolitical form like a cult. We have focused on the labor movement's internal character as well as relevant external conditions in accounting for the crystallization and subsequent political and organizational transformation of the May protest.[13] This emphasis has enabled us to see some other important implications of this case study, which we should mention at this point.

SIGNIFICANCE OF INTERNAL CONFLICT

It was noted earlier that the labor movement in Curaçao had been for a long period characterized by fragmentation and internal conflict. There is a tendency to define such conflict as inevitably maladaptive for a social movement. However, our study supports the position taken by Gerlach and Hine that conflict in a movement is at times adaptive. They note, for example:

> When the success of movements is reported as having occurred "because of" rather than "in spite of" organizational fission and lack of cohesion, we have come to understand the nature of movement dynamics much more clearly. Organizational unity is functional in a steady-state social institution designed to maintain social stability and the status quo. Segmentation and "internecine dog-fighting" are functional in a social institution designed for rapid growth and the implementation of social change.[14]

The labor movement in Curaçao was jolted from its position of accommodation with long-established political patterns in the society and transformed into an instrument for social change in part because of the presence of competing groups. Had it not been for the presence of the more radical labor leaders, the moderate labor leaders might have been able to guide the labor movement through the crisis without significant change occurring within the movement itself, as well as the larger society. The moderate leaders of the important PWFC were goaded into a more militant course of action, that is, into supporting the strike during the early phase of the May Movement, by the radical leaders. Further, the PWFC leaders supported the May Movement out of concern for losing the control of their union to the more radical leaders since many of their members were clamoring for action. Our findings on this matter provide support for Zald and Ash's proposition that: ''Goal and tactic transformation of a MO [movement organization] is directly tied to the ebb and flow of sentiments within a social movement. The interorganizational competition for support leads to a transformation of goals and tactics.''[15] The May Movement was the first time that the PWFC had engaged in militant strike activity with other unions in Curaçao. This marked a clear shift in tactics for the organization. Finally, the presence of the radical leaders in the labor movement was directly related to the eventual political orientation that the May Movement took. Had it not been for these leaders, labor's innovative political role might never have materialized. The internal conflict within the labor movement, then, was in part responsible for its large-scale mobilization for action during the May Movement and transformation into an important political instrument.

SIGNIFICANCE OF STRUCTURAL SETTING

There is a broader issue of concern to students interested in the development and transformation of social movements other than whether their goals are economic, political, or otherwise. This is the question of what determines the degree of change they seek. Smelser, for example, distinguishes between norm-oriented and value-oriented movements. Norm-oriented movements are those which call for only normative or reformative changes in a society, whereas value-oriented movements are those which demand more sweeping or revolutionary changes involving the very values of a society.[16] And according to Smelser, particular structural settings facilitate the formation of either norm-oriented or value-oriented movements.

Despite the use of the term *revolution* by many of the participants in the May protest in Curaçao, it was never transformed into a revolutionary movement. It began as and retained the character of a norm-oriented movement. This can be in part attributed to the nature of the social setting in which the May protest emerged, or more specifically to aspects of the social control situation. Thus our findings support Smelser's general proposition that the operation of social control is a major determinant of the form a social movement will assume. Smelser suggests that two social control factors facilitate the development of a norm-oriented movement and help it to retain this character during its existence: (1) a high degree of institutional differentiation,[17] and (2) the general encouragement of norm-oriented activities by political authorities and the opening of channels for the expression of grievances and achievement of normative changes.[18] Regarding the first point, Smelser suggests that in the absence of a high degree of institutional differentiation there is a tendency for demands initially made by a movement for limited and normative changes to generalize into demands for broader and more revolutionary kinds of changes. He notes, for example:

> In a society with a fusion between religious and political authority—many medieval societies could serve as examples— protest against specific normative arrangements inevitably tend to generalize into heresies. Under such conditions the mechanisms for insulating specific demands from challenges to legitimacy itself are not highly developed.[19]

In Curaçao, there appeared to have been less differentiation between the political and economic spheres than in more developed societies. This structural feature was one of the reasons why the May protest broadened to include political as well as economic demands. However, perhaps from the standpoint of social control, a more important form of institutional differentiation did exist in Curaçao which appears to have been involved in preventing the May Movement from becoming a value-oriented movement. That is, in Curaçao, there was a clear separation between the government in power and the *system* of government. Thus, in order to change the former, which constituted normative change, the latter did not have to be changed or threatened, which would have constituted radical change. When the coalition of unions went before the Staten and demanded that the government resign, they were attacking the policies of the government in power rather than the legitimacy of the system of government itself. That government officials also saw and accepted this distinction was indicated by the fact that they resigned. Thus this differentiation prevented the need for labor to seek a modification in the basis for the legitimacy of the political system itself in order to change the government's economic policies.

Finally, Smelser's proposition that the opening of channels for the expression of grievances and the achievement of normative change will encourage a norm-oriented movement to remain as such is also supported by the findings of this study. For example, after the government in Curaçao was toppled and a special election was set for September 5, the interim government permitted the formation of the May 30 Labor and Liberation Front and recognized it as a legitimate political party. This was the case in spite of the role the founders of the new party had played during the crisis and the charges that had been brought against them. The response by the government had the effect of providing the radical leaders the opportunity to use more traditional or legitimate means for bringing about desired change in the society. Thus the protestors were not forced to work outside the established system or underground in a revolutionary or insurrectionary movement. Indeed, some of the supporters of the new party wanted to work outside the government. However, because the party was given the opportunity to do so by the government, those who preferred to work within the system prevailed. Furthermore, after the September elections, the new government became more open to contacts with labor leaders in an effort to reduce the latter's sense of isolation and in recognition of their increased power. As Smelser suggests would be the case, such responses by political authorities facilitated the nonrevolutionary character of the May Movement.

1. Among others, Coser has noted that one of the consequences of external conflict for a group may be increasing internal solidarity. Lewis A. Coser, *The Functions of Social Conflict* (New York: The Free Press, 1962).

2. Sidney C. Sufrin, *Unions in Emerging Societies: Frustration and Politics* (Syracuse: Syracuse University Press, 1964), p. 24.

3. Structural conduciveness refers to the permissiveness in a given social structural setting of the development of a particular type of collective action. Neal J. Smelser, *Theory of Collective Behavior* (New York: The Free Press, 1962), p. 15.

4. Lucian W. Pye, "The Politics of Southeast Asia," in *The Politics of the Developing Areas,* ed. Gabriel A. Almond and James S. Coleman (Princeton: Princeton University Press, 1960), p. 116.

5. Martin Oppenheimer, *The Urban Guerilla* (Chicago: Quandrangle Books, 1969), p. 36.

6. For a discussion of the role of social control as it relates to the escalation of violence, see Smelser, *Theory of Collective Behavior,* especially pp. 261–69.

7. *Amigoe di Curaçao,* May 31, 1969.

8. Ibid., July 24, 1969.

9. *Beurs-en Neuwsberichten,* June 2, 1969.

10. Joseph R. Gusfield, "The Study of Social Movements," in *International Encyclopedia of the Social Sciences* 14 (New York: Macmillan, 1968), p. 447.

11. Blanksten has noted that the political or general strike has been used with frequent success in underdeveloped countries in Latin America. He writes, for example, "Since the 1930s the general strike has come to be a movement of growing importance in Latin America. Having more of an organizational base than the anomic movements discussed here, the general strike usually rests on labor unions and associations of university students, frequently acting in coalition. The general strike is especially important in Central America, where it has been a major factor in the overthrow of governments, particularly in Guatemala, El Salvador, and Honduras." George I. Blanksten, "The Politics of Latin America," in *The Politics of the Developing Areas,* ed. Gabriel A. Almond and James S. Coleman (Princeton: Princeton University Press, 1960), p. 498.

12. Oppenheimer writes, for example: "Members of the subordinate culture suffering various kinds of strain move away; they go abroad to a university. . . . Everywhere they come into contact with new ideas, frequently revolutionary ideas. They return home to infuse a proto-revolutionary movement with modern political, nationalist, revolutionary ideas." Oppenheimer, *The Urban Guerilla,* p. 39.

13. For examples of students who have recognized the importance of both internal and external forces in the transformation of social movements see: Mayer Zald and Roberta Ash, "Social Movement Organizations: Growth, Decay, and Change," *Social Forces* 44:327–41; and Harold A. Nelson, "Leadership and Change in an Evolutionary Movement: An Analysis of Change in the Leadership Structure of the Southern Civil Rights Movement," *Social Forces* 49 (March 1971): 353–71.

14. Luther P. Gerlach and Virginia H. Hine, *People, Power, Change: Movements of Social Transformation* (Indianapolis: Bobbs-Merrill Co., 1970), p. 64.

15. Zald and Ash, "Social Movement Organizations," p. 333.

16. Smelser, *Theory of Collective Behavior,* p. 272.

17. Ibid., p. 280.

18. Ibid., p. 307.

19. Ibid., p. 280.

# CHAPTER FIVE

## The May Movement and Social

## Change and Reform in Curaçao

The rise of the May Movement resulted in many changes in Curaçao. Some of these were the kinds of changes groups in the movement had hoped to achieve, while others were unintended consequences of their actions.[1] The changes, both intended and unintended, involved many aspects of the society. For the purpose of organizing our discussion, we can roughly categorize them as political, economic, and sociocultural changes. In this chapter, we will discuss the major changes in the political, economic, and sociocultural areas that emerged in Curaçao over a two-year period as a result of the May Movement.

POLITICAL CHANGE AND REFORM

Since the May protest evolved into a political movement, it is not surprising that the most significant changes it generated involved politics. As a new political force, the May Movement disrupted established political arrangements and led to the formation of new political organizations and power alignments. With their new-found power, groups participating in the May Movement were able to wrest concessions from other political and interest groups. At the same time, however, those most affected by the increased power of the newer groups resorted to such tactics as forming alliances and mergers in order to restore some of their lost power. The May Movement also furthered the development of factions and splits in some political and interest groups in Curaçao.

The most obvious political change wrought by the May Movement was the collapse of the central government and the success of the new labor party at the polls in the special September election. The significance of this turn of events was that the almost total domination of the central government by the Democratic Party of Curaçao came to an end. This did not mean that the Democratic Party was no longer a significant force in Antillean politics, because it still was. What it did mean, though, was that it could no longer afford to flagrantly ignore the need for supporting some government reforms and responding to some of the grievances of labor.

The Democratic Party had been able to remain in power, thus selecting the prime minister from its own ranks and dominating the selection of cabinet ministers, by forming a majority block with three parties from other islands. Prior to the May Movement, the seats in the Staten were divided as shown in table 4.

As the Democratic Party of Curaçao became more entrenched in the central government over the years, it became increasingly indifferent to certain political and interest groups, including labor. Opposition parties complained of being ignored by the Democratic Party in matters they felt they should have been consulted on as members of the Staten. At the same time, the opposition was

TABLE 4

SEATS HELD IN THE STATEN
PRIOR TO THE MAY MOVEMENT

| Party | Seats |
| --- | --- |
| *Democratic Block* | |
| Democratic Party of Curaçao ........................... | 7 |
| Patriotic Party of Aruba ............................... | 4 |
| Democratic Party of Bonaire ........................... | 1 |
| Democratic Party of the Windward Islands ................ | 1 |
| Total ................................................ | 13 |
| *Opposition* | |
| National People's Party of Curaçao ..................... | 5 |
| Aruban People's Party ................................. | 4 |
| Total ................................................ | 9 |

unable to organize and offer an effective alternative political program and approach. The Democratic Party was also criticized for engaging in excessive political favoritism when selecting persons to fill vacant public offices and in other matters.

The ruling Democratic Party became especially isolated from the labor unions. Although the party appealed to and received extensive support from labor unions and workers, many union leaders could see little benefit that the workers received from giving such support. There was criticism that the Democratic Party followed a program of economic development that benefited foreign investors or white locals rather than the average Antillean, while at the same time taking no effective action to improve inadequate social services. There were also no means whereby the labor unions could make an input into the government's economic decision-making process, even though decisions were being made that directly affected them.[2]

Why, then, had the Democratic Party continued to receive widespread voter support from workers in Curaçao? Part of the reason seems to be that since Kroon and others in the Democratic Party had helped to organize the PWFC, many workers still saw them as sympathetic to their cause, in spite of the apparent failure of the party to develop concrete programs beneficial to them. Also, given the personalistic feature of Antillean politics, people tended to give a great deal of attention to a politician's style, what he said, and the small favors he could dispense rather than such things as the type of legislation he sponsored. With a highly effective style, Kroon had acquired a large personal following and thus was able to attract considerable support for his party. Furthermore, until the May Movement and the formation of the Liberation Front, there was no party in Curaçao that seemed to offer a clear cut alternative to the Democratic Party. The National People's Party of Curaçao did not differ significantly from the ruling Democratic Party, and the newer URA party, after initially offering some promise, proved not to be significantly different either.

The Liberation Front's success at the polls in the special September election took away the Democratic block's majority. The

Democratic Party of Curaçao lost one seat to the Liberation Front and the Democratic Party of Bonaire lost its seat to a combination of two small parties. As shown in table 5, this meant that both the opposition parties and Democratic block had eleven seats in the Staten.

In the Antilles, parties with a combined total of at least twelve seats must reach an agreement to work together before a new central government can take office, and over two months of negotiations were required following the September election before a coalition government could be formed. The Liberation Front was asked to participate in the formation of the new government, and while there was strong opposition to this from some party members, it, nevertheless, became a part of a new coalition government that controlled a majority of fifteen seats in the Staten. In addition to the Liberation Front, the coalition included the parties that had previously made up the Democratic block, with the exception of the Democratic Party of Bonaire, which had lost its seat, plus the Bonairean Labor Party–United Progressive Bonairean Party. Thus, paradoxically, the Liberation Front found itself in the same government with the Democratic Party of Curaçao, one of the principal targets of the May Movement. This course of action was justified by those in the new party who

TABLE 5

SEATS HELD IN THE STATEN
AFTER THE SPECIAL SEPTEMBER ELECTIONS

| Party | Seats |
|---|---|
| *Democratic Block* | |
| Democratic Party of Curaçao | 6 |
| Patriotic Party of Aruba | 4 |
| Democratic Party of Bonaire | 0 |
| Democratic Party of the Windward Islands | 1 |
| Total | 11 |
| *Opposition* | |
| National People's Party of Curaçao | 3 |
| Aruban People's Party | 4 |
| Labor and Liberation Front of May 30 | 3 |
| Bonairean Labor Party–United Progressive Bonairean Party | 1 |
| Total | 11 |

supported it on the basis that as a member of the ruling coalition the party would be in a position to push for policies and programs beneficial to workers. Others in the party felt, however, that it could be more effective as part of the opposition, and that joining a coalition that included the Democratic Party meant a turning away from the principles of the May Movement.

The parties forming the new coalition met in Bonaire in November, 1969, where they drew up a set of principles called "The Agreement of Kralendijk" (see Appendix A) and also divided up the duties of government. The Liberation Front was assigned the portfolios for two ministries, social affairs and public health. The party selected Nita to fill the social affairs post, while someone else was to be later appointed to the public health post. The new government created a new department of labor, which also came under the direction of Nita as minister of social affairs. The labor department was established in response to grievances articulated by the labor unions during the May protest. Some of the matters that social affairs and the new department of labor were expected to deal with were the possible passage of a regulation setting a minimum wage for all laborers, the revision of labor legislation, and the formation of a committee consisting of representatives of labor unions to advise the government on labor matters. Soon after the new government was formed, Nita organized an advisory committee of labor leaders. Slight progress was made on labor legislation and considerable controversy was generated over the setting of a minimum wage. More will be said about this later.

In the new government, Kroon was replaced as prime minister by E. O. Petronia of the Patriotic Party of Aruba. The selection of the highly successful businessman made him the first black to occupy this office. This development was widely viewed as a response to the criticism made by May Movement groups that the government did not provide opportunities for blacks to hold high office. The appointment of a black man as governor of the Antilles by the kingdom government was likewise thought to be the result of pressure by those in the May Movement to increase the involvement of blacks in the ruling circle.

The May Movement led to some significant developments within the Democratic Party of Curaçao. One of them centered around party leadership. An internal power struggle had been brewing in the party prior to the May Movement between a group of long-time leaders and a faction of younger members. Kroon represented the party's old guard; he along with such men as Jonckheer, whom he had succeeded as prime minister and party head, and Isa had led the fortunes of the party for over twenty years. A younger group of party members, led by Rozendal who held a seat in Curaçao's Island Council, wanted greater influence in party affairs. This group used the May unrest as an opportunity to oust Kroon from the top position in the party.

Kroon, who had been opposed to the participation of the Liberation Front in the new government, wanted to be reinstated as prime minister. However, the new coalition refused to do so because he was so identified with those things which had led to the May Movement and the political crisis. Thus Petronia was selected as prime minister instead and the Liberation Front was admitted into the new government. These developments weakened Kroon's position in the Democratic Party and in July, 1970, the younger faction was able to oust him and install Rozendal as party head. This later led to Kroon's departure from the party.

Political stability did not return to Curaçao and the Antilles with the formation of the new government. In fact the political situation remained in a state of flux at least for the next two years. The central government underwent several crises and cabinet changes, and little legislative work was accomplished in spite of the many vital issues raised by the May Movement.

As was to be often the case, the Liberation Front was at the center of the first major crisis the new government had to face. There was opposition within the new majority coalition over the inclusion of the Liberation Front in the government. Many of the established politicians did not feel that the leaders of the new party were qualified to deal with the affairs of government or offered the proper image. Of the three Liberation Front leaders who occupied seats in the Staten, only Brown had had extensive formal education. Godett was uneducated, and a laborer, and had a poor command of Dutch, the language in which government affairs were conducted. He had the reputation of being a street brawler as well as a radical labor leader. The radical political views of Brown and Nita also threatened some of the politicians, and others were displeased because all three men wore the khaki dress that had become symbolic of Third World revolutionaries. The three leaders were also seen as instigators of the violence that had rocked Curaçao on May 30, 1969, and both Brown and Godett had spent time in jail in connection with the violence. Nita was thought to be less unacceptable by the coalition than Godett or Brown, and so when the Liberation Front offered him as its representative in the cabinet he was approved.

On June 17, 1970, several months after the new cabinet had been formed, the forty-nine-year-old Nita unexpectedly died. The Liberation Front claimed that he had been poisoned by enemies of the party and demanded that the government obtain the services of doctors outside the country to perform an autopsy. The prime minister agreed to the autopsy and doctors were brought in from Venezuela and Cuba who subsequently concluded that Nita had died of natural causes.

After Nita's death, Godett was proposed by the Liberation Front as his replacement as minister of social affairs but the coalition rejected him because of his lack of education and arrest record. Brown, too, was rejected on the basis of his criminal record. After rejecting both Godett and Brown, the coalition attempted to form a national cabinet—that is, one in which all parties were represented. It was felt that this was needed because of the recent unrest. The idea was to forget party differences and pull together for three years until the next election. Negotiations toward this goal ended in failure, however. The coalition then began negotiations with the National People's Party of Curaçao with the aim of including it in the cabinet. Thus in July, 1970, the National People's Party entered the cabinet and was given the portfolios of social affairs and public health that had been assigned to the Liberation Front up until the death of Nita.

During the negotiations for forming a new cabinet, the Liberation Front was very indecisive. This partly stemmed from the party's lack of political experience. It was also related to the fact that the young party was divided over the advisability of being a part of the ruling regime. One faction was for remaining in the cabinet in order to reap the immediate rewards of a party in power, such as appointments and other favors. Another faction, however, thought in terms of broader goals such as ultimate autonomy from Holland and a socialist order, and believed that the best way of achieving them would be to serve as a voice of protest outside the majority block until the voting masses had shifted their allegiance to the party, enabling it to take over the machinery of government. This internal division within the Liberation Front resulted in its announcing that it would accept an invitation to remain in the cabinet at one point and then announcing that it had no intention of doing so at another. The Liberation Front did finally decide to rejoin the cabinet, submitting the name of a party member who was acceptable to the rest of the coalition to represent it as a minister. Thus in August, 1970, the Liberation Front was again a member of the ruling coalition that now also included the National People's Party.

The next governmental crisis was triggered over legislation related to a wage increase for government employees. The May Movement led to considerable pressure for increasing wages in Curaçao and for establishing a minimum wage. As a member of the Island Council of Curaçao before becoming the executive head of the Democratic Party, Rozendal had proposed legislation for a wage increase for all government employees. In December, 1970, Petronia attempted to get legislation passed for an increase in wages for government employees, which was similar to the earlier proposal made by Rozendal to the island government. The legislation also called for tax increases in order to finance the wage boost. Paradoxically, rather than supporting this legislation, Rozendal, who had become a minister in Petronia's cabinet, resigned along with two other ministers from the Democratic Party because they did not like the way the prime minister was running the government. The Liberation Front also came out against the prime minister's wage and tax legislation, and so he was forced to resign because the vote total was eleven for and eleven against his legislative program—a vote of no confidence. In failing to support Petronia, the Liberation Front voted against legislation that much of the labor movement favored.

The contradictory action by the Liberation Front was apparently related to the highly personal nature of politics in Curaçao. The party's decision to vote against wage and tax proposals was based to a large extent on personal rather than ideological considerations. Before the vote on the legislation, Godett had asked the coalition government to accept as a second minister from his party a man with whom he had developed strong personal ties. This candidate was subsequently rejected by the coalition on the grounds that he lacked the qualifications for such an office. This was followed by the Liberation Front's rejection of Petronia's legislation.

By the time the Liberation Front had withdrawn its support from Petronia, Stanley Brown had left the party as he had threatened to do if the party offered Godett's choice for minister to the coalition. Like the members of the coalition who refused to accept him, Brown also strongly felt that Godett's candidate was ill-prepared to assume the duties of a cabinet minister. Thus Godett's action, based more on personal rather than political concerns, led to the departure of one of the party's most able and articulate spokesmen.

Because he opposed legislation similar to what he had himself strongly advocated earlier and was identified with much of the party's in-fighting, Rozendal became a political liability for the Democratic Party. As one party member put it, "He was doing the party too much harm." As a result, Rozendal was ousted from his position as party leader. Isa, one of the old guard members, became the new party head and in February, 1971, the new prime minister. Thus the old leadership within the Democratic Party, with the exception of Kroon, reestablished itself after being out for a short period. Under Isa's leadership, the legislation that had been rejected when Petronia presented it was passed with few changes.

In addition to the general political instability we have just described, the May Movement was responsible for the merging of two parties and the formation of two new ones besides the Liberation Front. Both the National People's Party and URA suffered political setbacks as a result of the protest vote received by the Liberation Front in the 1969 central government election. The National Party lost two seats in the Staten, and its leaders blamed this on the racial appeals the Liberation Front had made to workers. Nor did URA, contrary to its expectations, do well in the special national election. The party had won two seats in the first local election it had entered. It had received considerable support from labor and so its leaders anticipated doing well in the next national election. However, URA did not have anyone as closely identified with the May Movement and labor as the Liberation Front and so it received 2,000 fewer votes than it had received in the local election, five hundred less than the required total for winning a seat in the Staten. According to one URA party leader, "The Liberation Front got all the glory." The National Party and URA were hurt more by the Liberation Front than the Democratic Party because they were not as well organized and did not have as broad a base of support as the Democrats. Because the two parties had lost ground to the Liberation Front, they began thinking about the possibility of combining forces. Thus in October, 1969, they began merger negotiations. The merger became an accomplished fact in July, 1970.

The merger of the National People's Party of Curaçao and URA reflects the pragmatic and opportunistic character of politics in Curaçao.[3] One nonpolitician who was a government official described this opportunism in the following manner:

> Because of the lack of different ideologies, you very often see people going from one party to another. For example, you are a legislator from the Nationalist Party and suddenly you find it more comfortable to be in the Democratic Party, so you go to the Democratic Party. You see a lot of examples of this. This creates the tendency for the party that is well organized and in office to attract other people who are looking for power or for a better position and thereby always ending up stronger than they were.

The merger of the National Party and URA fits this pattern of political pragmatism. Only a few years earlier dissidents had left the National Party to form URA supposedly because of major ideological differences. The dissidents thought the leadership of the National Party was too conservative and so they sought to create a more radical alternative to both the National and Democratic Parties. Yet in only five years such differences were either forgotten or were seen as unimportant in the face of the more practical problem of dealing with the Liberation Front's challenge, and so the two groups reunited. Following the merger, the National People's-URA Party aimed for the upcoming May, 1971, island election.[4]

The two other parties that developed as a result of the May Movement were MASA and MAN. After being forced to resign as head of the Democratic Party, Kroon left the party and formed MASA. He had been groomed for several years to assume the leadership of the Democratic Party, and the formation of the new party enabled him to continue to pursue his political ambitions. At least one other former Democratic Party leader joined Kroon in his efforts to start the new party. Like the National People's-URA Party, the immediate goal of MASA was to win seats in the May, 1971, local election.

MAN was also organized before the 1971 island election. Its principal organizer was a young black government employee by the name of Donald Martina who believed that the Liberation Front had lost the initiative and thus a new party was necessary to fulfill the promises of the May Movement. Martina felt that the things his party would offer, which the Liberation Front could not, were the leadership skills necessary for operating in established politics and an unwillingness to compromise on the principles of the May Movement. MAN saw laborers as a major potential source of support, but race was the single most important issue for the party and it appealed exclusively to Antilleans of African descent, unlike the Liberation Front which also sought backing from progressive and radical whites. Some of the candidates offered by MAN in the May, 1971, local election had previously run for office on the Liberation Front's list.

Political leaders in Curaçao saw the approaching May, 1971, local election as very important. It was occurring two years after the May 30, 1969, unrest, the fall of the central government, and the birth of the Liberation Front. It was believed that the results of the local election would provide an indication of whether or not the Liberation Front was a viable political party and show to what degree the May Movement still existed or had a political impact. Furthermore, the emergence of MASA and MAN and the merging of the National Party and URA offered a whole new dimension to the election.

The results of the election are given in table 6. In the previous island election when there were only 3 parties offering candidates, the Democratic Party had won 13 of the 21 seats in the Island Council, and the National Party and URA, at this time separate parties, won 6 and 2 seats respectively.

As shown in table 6, the Liberation Front won 3 seats in the Island Council and MAN won one seat. These 4 seats represented the protest vote and indicated that the May Movement still had some impact on politics in Curaçao. The Democratic Party fell from 13 to 7 seats due to competition from the new parties, especially MASA, which won 3 seats; Kroon was able to attract some of the voter support to MASA that he had when he was in the Democratic Party. The National People's-URA Party acquired one seat less than the combined total they had won as separate parties in the previous election. Following several weeks of deliberation after the election, the Democratic Party and National People's-URA Party formed a coalition island government.

The island election, like the central government election that preceded it, reflected the flux in Curaçao politics following the May Movement. The history of Curaçao is replete with the

TABLE 6

RESULTS OF 1971 CURAÇAO ISLAND COUNCIL ELECTION

| Party | Seats |
|-------|-------|
| Democratic Party | 7 |
| National People's-URA Party | 7 |
| Liberation Front | 3 |
| MASA | 3 |
| MAN | 1 |
| Total | 21 |

emergence of new political groups, alliances, factions, and splits. In the past, however, such changes have emerged gradually, so the island was not accustomed to the extensive changes that the May Movement so suddenly produced.

During Curaçao's recent history, many new political parties have emerged and then disappeared without making a significant impact on the society. Many of them had offered alternative political programs during their quest for office but were unable or unwilling to follow through on them later. Since politics in Curaçao are so personal and opportunistic, the initial intentions of parties to make changes and solve problems have often been set aside to fulfill personal obligations and to remain in power. One observer expressed his disappointment with URA in this regard: "URA had a lot of intellectuals in it, looked very promising at the start. They were ideological and were supposed to break through this system of personal relationships, but they didn't manage it." Curaçao may not be very different from many other societies in this regard, except that due to its small size such patterns become more obvious.

Given its prior history, then, it might be that the political changes generated in Curaçao by the May Movement and reflected in both the 1969 and 1971 elections will be fairly short-lived. For example, like many small parties before them, the Liberation Front and MAN could disappear from the political scene, or, given the opportunistic nature of politics, they could attempt to broaden their base of support by toning down their protest, or, as URA did, even merge with a more established party. Even if any of these things occurred, however, politics in Curaçao will hardly be the same as they were prior to the May Movement because the political parties know that it has released a new consciousness among the black masses that they could ignore only at their own peril. The political parties realize that as a result of the May, 1969, violence and subsequent events the labor unions and black masses now have some awareness of their potential political strength. The politicians also know that they have become more cognizant of their rights, the social and economic disparity between their lives and those of whites, and that they have acquired a somewhat greater appreciation for their racial identity. Both the Liberation Front and MAN have helped to bring these things to the fore, and they are not likely to altogether disappear regardless of what happens to these two parties.

In addition to the political changes already discussed, the May Movement led to a number of attempts at political reform. The labor movement especially benefited from the new reform mood that grew out of the violence of 1969. In Coser's terms, the violence was a danger signal that called attention to the need for political and other kinds of changes in Curaçao.[5] In this context, the labor unions acquired considerably more influence and attention from the government and other sectors of the society than they ever had before. The unions were asked to participate on a number of civic boards for the first time. Government showed more interest in the activities of labor unions and significantly increased its consultation with them on matters related to its economic policy. In the past, the unions could only hope for favors from the government, having no way of influencing government decision-making. Mention has already been made of the creation of a labor department by the central government after the emergence of the May Movement. The central government also reconstituted a once defunct social and economic advisory council and appointed labor leaders to it in addition to leaders from the business sector. This was done so that labor leaders and others outside government could have an input in the setting of economic policies and reforms. One high government official in the Democratic Party characterized the council before the reform as, "the government advising government, dominated by the government." Finally, the government attempted to give greater recognition to the unions by inviting labor leaders to official functions and activities. This was seldom done before the May Movement.

Pressure from the protest movement forced the government to be more flexible in other ways. There was a significant lessening of the more blatant forms of favoritism when it came to making government appointments. It became more possible for people outside the ruling circle to be appointed to government posts. There was less hesitancy to appoint blacks to high office. We have already mentioned, for example, that blacks were selected as prime minister and governor. On the local government level, a black was appointed lieutenant governor; the duties of this office include heading up the police department in Curaçao. Those in power also showed a greater tendency to consider the opposition parties and to include them in important activities. This was seldom considered necessary before the May Movement. In general, there was a breakdown of some of the secrecy and isolation that had characterized government prior to the May Movement.

Along with the various reforms, another governmental response to the May Movement were efforts to strengthen the police and voluntary corps, the local militia. The police received heavy criticism following the May 30 uprising, especially from political opponents of the Democratic Party. The police were very indecisive when the violence erupted, and much of the blame for this was heaped on the lieutenant governor who had been appointed to his post by the Democratic Party even though he had had no previous police experience. Following the barrage of criticism, the Democratic Party removed the lieutenant governor from office and replaced him with a man who had considerable background in police work. Experts were also requested from the Netherlands to reorganize the police department. Police officers were given increased riot training, new riot squads were formed, and changes were made in written riot plans. The police felt that after May 30, citizens were more conscious of their rights, and so in training their personnel a new emphasis was placed on the need to be flexible and, as they put it, to use "psychology." The size of the police department's intelligence force was also expanded in order to increase its ability to gather information related to political activity. And the police department installed new communication equipment and acquired such things as antiriot guns and helmets.

As a result of the May Movement, the voluntary corps was given more formalized riot-control responsibilities. It was designated as a "secondary police force." A riot plan was written and corps members were given riot training for the first time. The new responsibility of the corps during social upheavals included guarding key public buildings and installations such as those related to water, electric, and telephone service. To the groups that had participated in the May Movement, these changes in the social control agencies were the unanticipated and undesirable consequences of their protest activities.

ECONOMIC CHANGE AND REFORM

With a few exceptions, employers and the business interests in Curaçao had taken workers and labor unions rather lightly. Since most of the unions were in a fairly weak bargaining position, given their lack of organization and resources, there was a great tendency for the unions, as they had done with the government and political parties, to seek favors from employers rather than contractoral agreements. However, after the May 30 upheaval, unions began to increasingly make demands of employers as they had done with the government.

There was an unprecedented upsurge in union membership and involvement after May 30. One high official attributed this to the fact that "the ordinary worker became conscious that he was a power in the community." The CFW illustrates the growth in union membership. Before May 30, it had approximately 1,200 members and by July, 1970, it had more than doubled to around 3,500 members. The emergence of four new unions in Curaçao was also the direct outgrowth of the new mood created by the May Movement.

Buoyed by their actions and success during the May crisis and by their expansion afterwards, the unions became increasingly militant. The unions, especially their rank and file, saw those who might oppose them as divided and weakened as a result of the May Movement. The older and newer unions negotiated an exceptionally large number of wage increases with employers who were often afraid to turn them down. There was also an increase in the number of wildcat strikes as workers began demanding rights as never before. Such a strike was even called against the government and eventually resulted in a substantial raise for blue-collar government employees.

In addition to granting pay increases, employers in Curaçao also responded to the May Movement by attempting to become more Antillean. Shell, for example, began putting emphasis upon replacing foreign staff members in technical and managerial positions with Antilleans. The company also started offering courses in Papiamento for its non-Antillean employees. In order to increase the number of skilled workers in Curaçao so that such persons would not have to be recruited outside the Antilles, a training program was organized by WESCAR, Shell, and the island government. Two years after the May upheaval, which gave birth to it, the program was in full swing.

Some employers in Curaçao took the position that a lack of communication and understanding between management and workers was at least partially responsible for the May violence. Thus they provided human relations and sensitivity training for their personnel. Companies like Shell and WESCAR also attempted to reduce ambiguity as a possible source of labor-management conflict by more clearly specifying company rules and regulations[6] and by setting up more periodic and formal meetings with employee groups.

Changes occurred between as well as within companies as a result of the May Movement. As others have noted, employers often respond to an apparent consolidation of labor unions by consolidating themselves.[7] The increased power and, for a time, unity of the labor movement served as the impetus for some companies in Curaçao to join and strengthen company associations. WESCAR, for example, joined an association of contracting companies after the May 30 upheaval. The Curaçao Employers Association, to which Shell belonged, was loosely organized prior to the labor crisis, but afterwards it was reorganized and given more attention by member companies in order to enhance their capacity for making joint decisions and taking common courses of action on labor and other matters.

The May Movement also served as the catalyst for the establishment in Curaçao of a public investment organization, the Curaçao Development Corporation (CODECO). The goal of the corporation was to get as broad a representation as possible—for example, those from labor, government, business, and the public-at-large—to work toward and invest in the industrial and business development of Curaçao. After a promotional campaign in July, 1970, shares in the corporation were sold to various organizations and private citizens. The cost of shares was kept low to permit their purchase by the average worker in Curaçao and thus hopefully provide this segment of the population with a sense of having some stake in the economic life of the island.

Paradoxically, as the unions began making gains, the solidarity that they had exhibited during the first several months of the May Movement began to wane. The old rivalries and differences that had previously kept them apart began to reappear. This was especially true of the Free and Christian unions. For example, a new union center with modern facilities was established in Curaçao with governmental assistance and contributions from unions in Holland. The center was supposed to be for the use of all labor unions in Curaçao, but the AVVC and CCV unions could not agree to work together and so it became primarily an AVVC facility. AVVC and CCV unions also began to bitterly compete over organizing workers. In one instance in early 1970, around 1,300 blue-collar workers left the AVVC-affiliated ABVO and formed a new union and then became affiliated with the CCV. Yet some gains continued to be made by labor even as it began showing signs of disunity. This was because the message received from the May 30 crisis by the business as well as the political community was that the violence could conceivably occur again if some changes were not made in the society.

SOCIOCULTURAL CHANGE AND REFORM

The history of slavery and colonialism in Curaçao has left its mark on the island in many ways. One of the most significant consequences of this history is that there is a tendency, as in other societies with similar experiences, for Antilleans to view black ancestry as undesirable. Thus the least amount of black physical traits a person has, the better off he or she is considered to be. In Curaçao there is also ambivalence, especially among the upper classes, about Antillean culture. The long history of domination by the Dutch has led some Antilleans to believe that any local variation from what is considered Dutch culture is inferior. The May Movement brought some signs of change in these patterns, however.

Some Antilleans became more positive toward the local culture after May 30. For example, many Antilleans were less defensive about their local or native foods after the emergence of the May Movement and more restaurants began selling it. Also middle-class people who had been embarrassed by a sexually suggestive folk dance called tambu, which had at one time been outlawed by the Dutch but was kept alive by people in the rural area of Curaçao, began frequenting the places where it was performed following the May revolt.

The May Movement was widely interpreted in Curaçao as a significant achievement or victory for the black masses.[8] As a result, some persons acquired a new sense of racial identity and pride. Persons who previously had been hesitant about discussing their African ancestry publicly took note of it after May 30. For some Antilleans who had not previously participated in the May Movement, the reference to their racial affinity with those who had was their way of belatedly joining the movement.

Social activities and opportunities that had been severely limited for darker-skinned people in Curaçao also opened up more after May 30, especially for those in the middle class. "May 30 broke all barriers," observed one Curaçaon. It became easier for blacks to acquire membership in such social-service clubs as the Rotary. Also after May 30, the Catholic church involved black grass-roots leaders more in its activities and functions.

Prior to the May Movement, the social-service clubs in Curaçao had come under severe criticism from many quarters for their exclusiveness and lack of contribution to the general welfare of the island. However, the clubs were widely credited with establishing one of the most successful post-May 30 programs in Curaçao. Soon after the violent outburst, the Lions, Rotary, and Kiwanis groups set up a Joint Service Club Committee for the purpose of developing a program for improving the island. This resulted in an organization called Obra y Logra, which translated means work and achievement. Obra y Logra was structured on a committee basis and included groups that worked on educational programs using the mass media, provided movies for various organizations, translated foreign-language articles into Papiamento, and provided speakers through a speakers' bureau. The most enthusiastically received part of the organization's work was a weekly television program called "Confrontation" on which Curaçao's social problems, such as those which had contributed to the labor unrest, were discussed. Much of the success and popularity of this program was related to the fact that, unlike in the past, a cross section of the population was able to air its views on television. This medium is partly subsidized by the government and previously it had been difficult for those with views that differed from the government's to receive television time or coverage. Obra y Logra was given free time for its program.

The sociocultural changes were somewhat more subtle than the political and economic ones, but, as we have indicated, some identifiable sociocultural changes did occur. All the changes, of course, point out that Curaçao was a different social system than it had been before May 30, 1969.

THE SOCIETAL CAPACITY FOR REFORM

We have explained why the transformation in the labor movement occurred—that is, what factors led to the May Movement and its various phases. We have also attempted to explain why the May Movement assumed a particular form—that is, became a reform or norm-oriented movement rather than a revolutionary movement. Our present task is to account for the degree of success the May Movement had during the two-year period that this study was conducted.

As a reform movement, the May Movement sought political, economic, and sociocultural reforms. More specifically, it was aimed at securing greater political power for the masses, the majority of whom were black, to improve their economic lot, and to enhance their social status. The movement, as our previous discussion indicates, did achieve some reforms of this nature. The government, the business community, and other segments of the society did make some effort to reduce some of the social strain that had led to the dramatic actions by the unions. However, many *basic* political, economic, and social problems of the masses remained unchanged. The May Movement could only generate a certain degree of reform given its own characteristics and those in the social environment in which it had to operate.

Each society has a particular capacity for reform. During any given period there will be present both conditions that are conducive to reform and conditions that hinder or set limits to it. It is the interaction between reform-facilitating and reform-limiting conditions that determines a society's reform capacity. Important in this regard in Curaçao were dimensions of the May Movement, such as its leadership and integration, and various properties of the social structure of Curaçao including its economy, political system, and social-control capabilities.

*Facilitating Factors*

Several factors opened the way for reform in Curaçao, the main objective of the May Movement. First, there were the factors, previously alluded to, that gave the May Movement the capacity for exerting pressure for change. This included the presence of charismatic labor leaders around whom the May Movement could crystallize. These leaders gave the movement much of its cohesion and direction during its most successful period. The support labor in Curaçao received from other quarters, such as the unions in Aruba and various critics and opponents of the government and business community in Curaçao, was also important. The Aruban unions enlarged the power base of the May Movement and contributed to its success in deposing the central government. Several groups in Curaçao, including the opposition parties at one point, gave the movement moral support and increased the legitimacy of many of its demands for reform by denouncing the ruling Democratic Party and in some cases the practices of the business community. In the case of the political parties, as well as in other instances, such support was later withdrawn when the new labor party was formed and posed a threat to them. But this support still had been important, coming as it did during the May Movement's major drive for reform and on the heels of the May 30 violence. Without this support the government might not have stepped down.

Given the new-found power and militancy of the labor movement after the May 30 upheaval, certain structural conditions in Curaçao were also conducive to reform. There was always the possibility that renewed violence could have developed in Curaçao if some reforms had not been forthcoming. The government could hardly take a chance on this since the police had performed poorly in containing the May 30 violence and the voluntary corps was a small nonprofessional organization. Most societies would have regular military troops at their disposal for such emergencies, but it will be recalled that under the kingdom government arrangement the Netherlands controls all military forces. The likelihood of Curaçao again receiving military aid in the event of another outbreak of violence was highly questionable since the Dutch had been worried about world opinion and possible charges of neocolonialism and intervention even as they committed troops to Curaçao after the May 30 violence. And the fact that demonstrations had been held in the Netherlands protesting their actions made the Dutch even more sensitive about this issue. Thus the need to avoid more violence because of the government's uncertainty about its ability to contain it underscored the necessity for granting some reforms.

The factionalism within the Democratic Party also increased the opportunity for reform in Curaçao with the emergence of the May Movement. After the September election in 1969, members of the

Democratic Party's old guard, led by Kroon, wanted to prevent the new labor party from joining the new government coalition, but they were overruled by the then up-and-coming faction of younger party members led by Rozendal. Also, when Kroon was ousted from the leadership of the Democratic Party, the new ruling faction tried to disassociate itself from the old politics by being more open to labor and other groups. A unified Democratic Party might have doggedly resisted making such changes.

*Limiting Factors*

In spite of the promising changes the May Movement did bring to Curaçao, the basic issues it had initially raised remained unresolved two years after its emergence and there were signs pointing to the conclusion that the movement had lost the initiative it had so suddenly gained. The May Movement could not sustain its innovative role because it became limited by both internal and external factors. Let us first consider those obstacles that were internal to the labor movement, the major vehicle of the May Movement.

One of the main factors that eventually limited the capacity of the May Movement to initiate reforms in Curaçao was the inability of the labor movement to sustain the unity it had manifested from the time of the economic strike phase to the initial political party phase of the May revolt. The divisions that existed among many of the unions in Curaçao before the May Movement were so deep that when the most dramatic part of the confrontation with the government which had united them was over and labor was seen as victorious, the old rivalries and conflicts resurfaced. Gradually some unions began taking courses of action that indicated their belief that a weakened government and business community provided them the opportunity to make gains for their individual unions. The rivalries increased and some unions tried to make gains at the expense of sister unions. This individuation of union goals and actions, which was in full swing several months after the May 30 violence, meant that those forces which might be opposed to reforming Curaçao no longer had to face a united front of unions.

The nature of the May Movement's leadership, especially during the political party phase, was another internal factor that set limits on its capacity to function as an instrument for reform. The leadership requirements of a social movement vary with its level of development. During a movement's formative period, the charismatic type of leader may be best suited to meet its needs. At this point in its history, a movement tends to require leaders who can inspire and enlist the involvement of potential followers. No specialized organizational or administrative skills may be required of the leaders, only that they have the kind of style that can rally people to the cause.[9] Thus up until the political party phase of the May Movement, its core group of leaders, Godett, Brown, and Nita, had proved to be quite successful. This was not the case, however, when the Liberation Front was formed and began operating in the area of institutionalized politics. During this later phase of the May Movement, administrative and organizational skills were needed, but the leaders did not possess them and so they became less effective. The indecisiveness and inconsistency of the Liberation Front reflected, to a large degree, its leaders' lack of political organizational skill and experience.[10] Moving from the politics of protest and disruption to institutionalized politics meant that the leaders of the new party had to compete and bargain with professional politicians on the latters' terms rather than on their own. One respondent, in accounting for the Liberation Front's difficulty along these lines suggested, ''They are a movement which never crystallized into a party.''

The extent to which the Liberation Front could push for reforms was also limited by serious internal dissension. One faction, led by Brown, wanted the party to assume a protest style. The position was taken that in order to maintain the purity of its convictions the party should not join coalitions because this necessitated compromise. Another faction, led by Godett, believed that the party should focus on concrete objectives rather than ideology, and concluded that these could best be achieved by becoming included in the ruling coalition. The party moved in the direction preferred by Godett and, being a purist, Brown was highly critical of this development. At one point, writing in the newspaper *Vitó*, he publicly accused Nita of using his position as minister for his own personal gain and that of his close associates rather than for furthering the aims of the May Movement and the people of Curaçao. In the latter part of 1970, Brown left the party and resigned from his seat in the Staten, accusing Godett of allowing personal commitments to subvert the goals of the party and of permitting the ascendancy of opportunists who had originally opposed the party. When Brown departed from the party, leftists who had marginally supported it because of his presence also withdrew their support. This group had always been hesitant in becoming heavily involved in the Liberation Front anyway because of its lack of ideology. Brown's departure further weakened the party because he was one of its few educated leaders.

External factors also set limits on the changes and reforms that could be generated by the May Movement. This included the economic structure of the Antilles, which reflected its status as a developing society. After the May 30 uprising, it was proposed that a minimum wage of 80 guilders per week be set by the government for all workers in Curaçao. This would have represented a substantial increase for many workers; for example, many hotel employees, one of the major groups of employees on the island, were only earning 40 guilders per week. The proposal never became law, however, essentially because considerable opposition was generated against it based on Curaçao's economic situation. The Curaçao Chamber of Commerce was one of the most outspoken critics of the proposal and it published a study that suggested that Curaçao's economy, which is heavily dependent upon attracting foreign investors, would undergo a possibly fatal blow with the passage of the minimum wage provision. The study suggested that existing industries would be driven out of business, especially hard hit would be the labor-intensive industries like hotels, and the country would be at a severe disadvantage in the competition for new foreign investors. Some labor leaders also questioned the wisdom of an across-the-board 80-guilder minimum wage, fearing that it might ultimately result in a decrease in the number of jobs in Curaçao. Rather than passing what was considered by many to be an extreme measure, then, the government granted wage increases to government employees, and unions individually negotiated with employers for wage increases. Thus as a result of Curaçao's economic structure, wage increases were kept within certain limits.

The nature of Curaçao's political system also set limits to social reform. Politics in Curaçao are highly pragmatic and opportunistic. There is considerable wheeling-and-dealing by political parties, both inside and outside the public political scene, often at the expense of solving problems or making reforms. The emphasis is given to acquiring and maintaining influence. This lack of concern for reform is also reinforced by the personalistic nature of politics in Curaçao. Again it should be mentioned that there is the tendency for voters to react to a politician on the basis of his personal style and what he can do for them in the way of personal favors rather than his performance in office.[11] Partly because of this quality of politics in the Antilles, there has been little sustained impetus for change and reform.

New parties have emerged in Curaçao from time to time to challenge this situation only to find themselves submitting to it and assuming many of the characteristics they had originally sought to reform. This pattern continued after May 30. URA had been organized to offer an alternative to the opportunism and favoritism of the established parties. Yet it laid aside its idealism and concern for reform and merged with the National Party when they both were hurt at the polls by the Liberation Front. On its part, the Liberation Front had promised to oppose those parties which had for so long stood in the way of progress for workers. But when it was given the opportunity, it joined in forming a government with the Democratic Party, the party that it had earlier declared was most responsible for the plight of workers and blacks. In essence, the Liberation Front was co-opted by the established parties, and it too became caught up in the opportunistic and personalistic politics, thus seriously limiting the extent to which it could function as the catalyst for reform in Curaçao. The Liberation Front's co-optation into the opportunistic political system is mirrored in the advice one party leader gave to another: "We have won the revolution. Now let's enjoy it."

1. Merton, in his classic essay, uses the terms manifest and latent functions to help distinguish between intended and unintended consequences of social action. Robert K. Merton, *Social Theory and Social Structure* (New York: The Free Press, 1969), p. 114.

2. Sufrin notes the significance of this kind of situation. "Union leadership and membership should be integrated into the formulation of the economic plans and programs of the government. . . . Thus, the various types of social and economic legislation, representation on commissions, and other operations of the government should take into account the existence of trade unions and of their leadership. Few snubs are so devastating to the self-respect of union members and leadership as to be denied a place on a board or commission which deals with matters of wages, hours, and conditions of employment." Sufrin, *Unions in Emerging Societies: Frustration and Politics*, p. 69.

3. Blanksten's description of pragmatic parties fits the character of parties in Curaçao. "Pragmatic parties are those which make no major ideological or philosophical demands upon their membership. Such parties are far more interested in commanding votes than the minds of their followers, who may enter or leave them without undergoing the trauma of ideological, philosophical, or religious conversions." Blanksten, "The Politics of Latin America," p. 482.

4. Zald and Ash note that a true merger leads to the suppression of previous organizational identities and that they tend to occur when they offer the promise of increasing the chances of goal attainment for the parties involved. Zald and Ash, "Social Movement Organizations: Growth, Decay, and Change," pp. 327–41. In the case under discussion, the goal was the acquisition of power.

5. Lewis A. Coser, "Some Social Functions of Violence," *Annals of the American Academy of Political and Social Science* (March, 1966), p. 12.

6. Coser notes that Simmel suggests that conflict may act as a stimulus for the establishment of new rules and norms. Lewis A. Coser, *The Functions of Social Conflict* (New York: The Free Press, 1962), p. 124. We may add that social conflict may also serve as a stimulus for the clarification of existing rules and norms. After May 30, for example, WESCAR wrote a code specifying the rules of the company and what was expected of its employees.

7. Coser says, for example, "The act of unification, even on the elementary level of coalition or instrumental association calls forth some kind of unification of those other groups and individuals who feel themselves threatened by the coalition. Employers were moved by the threat of growing trade unions to ally themselves with other employers in order to combat the union 'menace.' The rise of trade unions stimulated the rise of various types of employers' associations." Ibid., p. 148.

8. Coser argues that violence may offer one of the few avenues for the oppressed in a society to achieve certain desired goals and a sense of dignity. "Some Social Functions of Violence," pp. 10–12.

9. Killian has aptly captured the style of the charismatic leader in the following passage. "He tends to be bold, even impulsive, given to the dramatic gesture and the stirring appeal to emotions. He is both prophet and agitator. He states the movement's

values in absolute terms, often through slogans. He exudes confidence and may propose novel, dramatic tactics which promise success for the movement against all odds. At the same time, he is a symbol of courage and of willingness to suffer martyrdom rather than compromise. This type of leader may appear impractical, idealistic, or even fanatical to the outsider. But he quickly assumes heroic proportions in the eyes of people already committed, even in part, to the values of the movement, and to many who are dissatisfied with the status quo but not yet committed to a specific program of change. He simplifies the issues, resolving the ambivalence which potential followers may feel." Killian, "Social Movements," p. 441.

10. Lipset and others do a good job of describing how the lack of experience and skill of its leaders limits a party once it comes to power. S. M. Lipset, et. al., *Agrarian Socialism* (Berkeley: University of California Press, 1950).

11. The term "personalismo" is often used in referring to this kind of political orientation. Blanksten notes, "Personalismo may be defined as the tendency to follow or oppose a political leader on the basis of his personality rather than on ideological grounds—to be swayed by personal, individual, and family motivations rather than by an impersonal political idea or program." Blanksten, "The Politics of Latin America," pp. 482–83.

# CHAPTER SIX

## The May Movement in the
## Context of Other Social Movements

In the previous chapters, we looked at the May Movement and its implications for social change in Curaçao. In this final chapter, we will place the May Movement in a larger context. We will first return to the question of the relation of the violent incident on May 30 to the totality of the May Movement. Such violent incidents are usually explained by theories that have little relationship to the nature of social movements. We wish to emphasize an explanation of the violence in Curaçao that places it as one aspect of a political process and also to suggest that, by the observation of the nature of violence, important clues as to the direction of protest can be derived. A second point that will be stressed, drawn from the Curaçao experience, is that labor movements are particularly significant in developing societies. There are certain developmental factors that make the work relationship especially critical in such societies and thus labor issues are likely to be at the heart of various social movements. A third issue to be examined are the similarities and differences between the May Movement and the black movements in the United States. Civil disturbances in Watts, Newark, Detroit, Cleveland, and many other American cities during the 1960s can also be seen as one part of the black protest movement in the United States, and it is instructive to examine this movement in relation to Curaçao. In addition to comparing the May Movement with similar efforts in the United States, it is also useful to attempt to put the May Movement in the larger context of social movements within the Western world. Was the May Movement unique or does it have continuities to other social movements? Finally, we will conclude with certain implications that the May Movement has for the future of Curaçao.

## THE NATURE OF VIOLENCE AND THE DIRECTION OF PROTEST

From the very beginning we have treated the violence that developed on May 30 as one phase of the May Movement. Although the continuity of the various stages of the movement may be obvious by now, it is perhaps necessary to add further support to the contention that the violence could be understood as a manifestation of protest. Violence associated with mass movements is often explained in other ways. One theory suggests that the vandalism, looting, and arson that occur are a result of deep-seated criminal tendencies which typify those attracted to a movement. (There is usually a racist implication in such theories.) Although these tendencies may most often be latent, under particular circumstances of crowd behavior, such criminal tendencies reassert themselves and are expressed in socially destructive ways. Another theory suggests that rioting can be fun. This theory implies that, given certain conditions where there is a lack of authority, certain elements in society will evidence a lack of self-discipline and self-control. The carnival-type atmosphere and the absence of visible authority in riots will provide the opportunity for a ''festive'' event in which self-control disintegrates and a whole range of deviant behavior emerges. A third rather common explanation resides in the ''outside agitator'' theory. This assumes that most persons are satisfied and are capable only of being made discontented by malcontents from outside the community. Given such outside agitation, the locals, stimulated by the crowd, are led to deviant behavior. Often when the vandalism and looting are recognized as having been selective, this is seen as the consequence of advance planning and preparation by the outside agitators. Jones and Molnar in a wide ranging examination of civil disorders in a variety of places and at different historical times note:

> Those in power have usually assumed that the rioters had no worthwile aspirations and could be motivated to activity only by the promise of reward from outside agitators or conspirators. Until the deeper aspirations of the poor began to be investigated their periodic rebellions and riots were often attributed to the manipulation of a political opponent or a ''hidden hand.'' This attitude has been so popular in history that it has been shared by all authority, regardless of whether the governing elite was aristocratic, middle class, conservative, liberal, or revolutionary.[1]

All of these theories were raised in Curaçao in the assessment of blame after the rioting on May 30.

As we have suggested, it is more useful to conceptualize violence as a part of the political process and as an aspect of more inclusive protest activities. In this view, the violence that did occur in Curaçao on May 30 can best be interpreted as communicating a message from an underclass to the larger society. Thus massive looting can be seen as one form of group protest. This perspective is consistent with recent interpretations of violence, particularly that associated with looting which occurred in the context of racial disturbances in American cities during the 1960s.[2] The evidence that has been derived from these situations suggest the following. In certain types of crowd situations, looting becomes widespread and looters come from all segments of the population, not just the criminal element. The looting is not done by outsiders nor by isolated opportunists. Looters often work in pairs, family units, and small groups. Its collective nature sometimes reaches the point where the availability of potential loot is called to the attention of bystanders or, in some instances, those not involved are handed goods by looters coming out of stores. The public character of looting is striking since goods are taken openly and in the full view of others—bystanders, coparticipants, and often even security forces. During this time there is not only little sanction *against* such behavior, there is even strong immediate support *for* it. The so-called carnival spirit that has often been noted is more appropriately seen as an indication of the degree of open collective support for such activity. In the American experience, consumer goods are often the target, and grocery, furniture, apparel, and liquor stores have been the primary objects of attack.[3]

The widespread incidence of this behavior in such situations and the social support for it seems to require an explanation that goes much beyond conventional notions of criminality. The most appropriate explanation, we feel, revolves around the complexities of the nature of property. The word *looting* comes from a military context that suggests taking of "goods and possessions." It is, however, more appropriate to see property as a set of rights rather than as a concrete thing or as a material object. As Gouldner and Gouldner suggest, "property consists of rights held by the individual . . . to certain valuable things, whether material or immaterial."[4] By rights, we mean shared expectations about what can or cannot be done with respect to something. In effect, property is the shared expectation about who can do what with the valued resources within the society. Normally such understandings or expectations are widely shared and accepted throughout a society. Many of the basic understandings become specified in legal norms that define the legitimate use and control of these resources. These understandings become "taken-for-granted" with the day-to-day activity in all societies. But they are also at the core of the dispute that we label as *disturbances*.

In such disturbances, the expectations that have been previously accepted change and there is a redefinition of property rights on the part of a significant part of the community. The traditional right to the use of available resources becomes problematic. If property is seen as shared understanding of *who can do what* with the valued resources, then in such situations there is a breakdown in this understanding. In this context, new norms emerge, temporarily or even momentarily, but these new norms have widespread support. Such widespread support makes law enforcement (or more correctly the old-norm enforcement) almost impossible. Enforcing laws that are violated by a few is not difficult but enforcing laws that everyone violates is impossible. At the height of such situations, looting becomes normative, the socially acceptable thing to do. This was evident when the march on May 30 entered the heart of the Willemstad business area. Instead of being deviant, looting became, in that immediate situation, conforming behavior to the new norms that had emerged. Of course, the legal right did not change, as governmental officials argued subsequently, but there was widespread consensus among the marchers on the ''appropriate'' use of goods and even on the appropriateness of certain merchants doing business.

It should be noted that whereas such shifts in property definitions change quickly, they also change back quickly. Although there was some violence at Post V prior to the beginning of the march, as well as some along the way, the primary looting and arson did not occur until after Papa Godett was shot. On the other hand, it is also likely that many of those who engaged in the looting and perhaps the arson also played a part in helping stop it. This is perhaps illustrated best by one incident that occurred in the late afternoon on May 30. A government official was attempting to reduce the firespread in the center of the city. As he was struggling with a fire hose, he called a passer-by for aid. The passer-by said, ''I'll be glad to help but you'll have to give me a minute to get used to my shoes.'' He sat down and flexed and stretched his recently looted shoes and then turned his attention for the next several hours in trying to put out the fire. The looter in one context was also a helpful citizen in another.

The events suggest that a new property norm emerged among the rioters and that their behavior was directed by this new norm. Thus, their behavior was not expressive—engaging in riotous behavior, just for fun—nor did their behavior reveal the emergence of repressed criminality. The fact that so many people were engaged in looting, vandalism and arson suggests the widespread support for the new norms.

Clues to the nature of the new norms that guided behavior can be detected in observing the pattern of damage that did emerge. The violence does, in fact, reveal the complexities of the issues in

Curaçao, since one, then another, theme became apparent. Certainly, at the outset, the issues were primarily economic. At the morning meeting at Shell, however, Papa Godett redefined the issues in political terms. When he suggested the march, the positive response to his suggestion was not solely a measure of his personal power because it was seen as an acceptable means of showing the solidarity that had been emerging among the workers over the previous several days. As the march started toward the source of political power, Fort Amsterdam, the initial looting seemed to be of the harassment type where consumer goods were taken. Along the way, one factory was entered and the workers somewhat harassed. The factory was a recently established one, Amercian owned. It had recently discharged workers and had been the target of union complaints. One of the first cars burned on the morning of May 30 belonged to a Dutchman who some years before had been accused of killing a black boy. That the courts had dealt with him "leniently" was a matter of common knowledge and complaint within the black community.

The confrontation with the police and the subsequent wounding of Papa Godett shifted the dimensions of the march to a more political establishment confrontation and the shooting illustrated in a vivid fashion to the marchers what traditionally happened to their complaints. After this confrontation, the remnants of the marchers moved into the downtown area where the major vandalism and looting took place. One can argue that the norm that was emerging and that guided subsequent behavior was one which suggested that "only those who identify with Curaçao have a right to control any of its resources." This was reflected in the targets of looting and is particularly underscored by the first store that was set on fire. It was a special target since the store had been one in which efforts to unionize had not been successful and its owners had a reputation of buying most of its inventory outside of the island. The owners were relative newcomers to Curaçao, or more correctly they were not among the older families, but they had become economically successful in a relatively short time. The fact that the store had been the focus of attention in *Vitó* a short time before the disturbance was seen as evidence of preplanning but it more likely indicates the widespread definition of "exploitation" that the store had gained. The fact that the fires were reset in the store after they had been initially suppressed underscores the symbolic importance that the store had in the protest.

The selectivity of the looting and arson was interpreted by some as the result of preplanning and ultimately as the work of outsiders. It seems clear to us that the leaders of the march were locals, not outsiders. The shooting of Papa Godett and his removal to the hospital accompanied by many of the other leaders left the remainder of the marchers without leadership. The selectivity of the subsequent damage seems to indicate the clarity certain targets had for those who were in the march. Since the march was initiated as a result of the interaction of the crowd and the speakers at Post V, and the confrontation with the police and the subsequent shooting was also not planned, the patterns that developed as a consequence of the actions of hundreds of individuals as they moved into the central business district suggest the rather widespread, in fact, almost universal definitions certain targets had for them. These definitions were positive as well as negative.

Just as it is important to look at the pattern of looting and destruction, it is equally important to look for those elements that were relatively untouched during the disturbance. If one assumes a probability model in reference to damage and assumes the various types of property, particularly in the line of march and in the vicinity of the greatest concentration of the mob, had an equal chance of being destroyed, there are rather striking patterns of omission. (Of course, one would not expect a perfect relationship. Firespread is often unselective while fire origins are often more indicative. Looting and vandalism can, of course, be opportunistic and idiosyncratic and, therefore "irrational.") It is interesting to note that, with some minor exceptions, no residences were burned. Neither were public buildings. It would seem that at least some damage would have resulted at Fort Amsterdam since this was the intended culmination of the march. Even taking into account the greater security measures there, this would not be sufficient to account for the total lack of attention. Other types of public and quasi-public buildings were ignored. Just prior to the confrontation between the marchers and the police as the latter moved toward downtown, the marchers peacefully filed past the Curaçao Red Cross Building without incident. Just after the shooting of Papa Godett, the majority of the mob passed the post office without creating significant damage. Destruction of other types of public property, such as fire engines and police cars, tended to occur only in the context of periodic confrontations with police.

The bulk of the damage then was in terms of commercial property, but there were also some interesting patterns of omission here. Immediately after passing the post office, the mob also passed Curaçao's famed floating market, where ships from Venezuela that bring fresh produce to the island were docked. These "foreign capitalists" did not become the focus of attention.

In addition, one of the most significant factors was the *lack* of damage to Shell property on the island. Both the gathering point for the start of the march and the initial phase of the march were in close proximity to Shell property. Various Shell properties, ranging from offices to gas stations, are scattered over the island and the lack of opportunity is not a sufficient explanation for the marchers' lack of attention. Even random destruction would have likely produced some significant losses for Shell. Instead, the destruction was directed toward other targets.

Although the disturbance was widely interpreted afterward in the press and on the island as being a black-white confrontation, this interpretation is true *only* to the extent that the whites were seen as an oppressor and as an outsider. The nature of Curaçao with its primarily white upper class and black under class, did of course, provide some basis for black-white confrontation. But the whites who suffered the most were those who were considered outsiders and exploiters. Whites who had been on the island a long time and, more importantly, were seen to identify with the island as citizens, rather than as visiting colonials, were seldom harmed. In the relatively small population of the island, these insiders versus outsiders were generally known. In a mass situation, however, accurate identification becomes difficult and misidentification can and did happen. "Correct" identification was often quickly achieved if the white could speak Papiamento, the local language. For example, after the initial escalation at Shell, a young white newspaper reporter was turned on by the crowd, but they were diverted by his ability to handle the local language. Also, during the initial stages of the march, a car was stopped and the driver, a young Dutch woman, was asked to get out. As she got out indignantly, she started swearing in Papiamento. At this, the crowd, which had been threatening her minutes before, broke out in laughter and someone quickly said, "Let her go, she's one of us."

The inside-outside dimension rather than the black-white dimension is further illustrated by the fact that much of the economic loss was suffered by merchants, primarily Askenazian Jews who were newcomers rather than Sephardic Jews who were long-term residents. Another example, which points to the outsider-insider dimension rather than to a purely racial confrontation, were the many instances of blacks leading white tourists who had been caught in the disturbance area back to their hotels to protect them from mistaken harassment.

It would seem that the message that was conveyed in the violent episode reinforced other themes that were present throughout the May Movement and thus should be considered an integral part rather than as something apart. The strongest focus of protest as it was revealed through the various forms of violence was directed toward those who were seen to exploit the island and its people without identifying with Curaçao. The major focus of hostility expressed was directed toward those who were defined as outsiders. This distinction was particularly significant to the workers since they felt that they were the real insiders, the real Antilleans, but they felt instead that they were being treated as outsiders, excluded from the economic and political resources that should be rightfully theirs. The complexities of the issues involved— political powerlessness, low economic status, and blackness—tended to become joined in the major symbol of Antillean identity. Those who identified, regardless of color, could be a party to the continuing discussion of what Curaçao was to become. Those who did not identify, as reflected in their previous actions and behavior, had no right to continue to control valued resources on the island. The point was made in a rather frightening way, but it had been made. Subsequently, there was considerable debate as to the costs of the message but as Chapter five suggests, the various segments on the island began to listen as they had not previously.

THE IMPORTANCE OF LABOR IN SOCIAL MOVEMENTS
IN DEVELOPING COUNTRIES

Certainly one of the striking aspects of the May Movement was the critical importance of labor in all of its phases. For a number of reasons, it seems that the role of labor in social movements may be more important in societies developing now than it was in the development of older industrial societies. First, the work relationship may be particularly critical within such societies once it is reflective of social strain. Second, the development of unions as an effective mechanism in resolving worker complaints is somewhat problematic. Third, the size of the labor force is attractive as a political base and tends to attract leaders who have aims directed toward broader political issues rather than to narrow economic goals.[5]

In developing societies, the work relationship may be a particularly sensitive indicator of social strain that eventuates in the emergence of social movements. One of the key transitions in developing countries involves the shifting of loyalties from such social units as the family or the village to other social units more closely tied to the changing economic base. The traditional social units lose their relevance for ordering life whereas other associations become more relevant. Since a universal goal of developing societies is increasing the industrial base, the number of jobs within the urban industrial sector increases and these jobs become key elements that connect individuals and families to the larger changes within the society. The worker's job satisfaction, his relationship with other workers and with his employer become particularly significant in his evaluation of both his own progress and the progress of the larger society. In the Western industrial experience, trade unions developed to mediate some of the problems that workers experienced as a result of industrialization. Although conflict often emerged when union objectives were sought, unions in many ways provided a stabilizing influence to the course of labor relations. In developing countries, there are a number of factors that may undercut the potential stabilizing effects unions have had in the older industrialized societies. In addition, there are factors that make union development more problematic. In many developing societies, industrial employers, particularly those that utilize a high proportion of unskilled labor, are not concerned with the development of a fixed identifiable group of workers. They are far more interested in having an easily accessible pool of workers that can be drawn upon when the need arises. When such a potential labor supply is easily available, the employer is free, within certain legal limits, to establish those work relationships he deems necessary. This frequently makes job tenure insecure and discipline erratic. Given such employment tenuousness in situations of marginal employment, any changes in job context, rules, regulations, and the like, are seen as extremely threatening by the workers.

The emergence of trade unions to cope with such worker problems is often slow in developing societies. Employers can easily find substitutes for troublesome employees. The traditional backgrounds from which the workers come provide little experience in the development and maintenance of such a complex form of social organization as the union. The structure of industry in developing countries often requires primary dependence on industrial unionism. The level of technology available now makes the construction of larger units possible and economic competition makes the construction of larger units necessary. Masses of workers are often drawn together in such enterprises, none of them having much previous industrial experience. By contrast, during the early stages in the older developed countries, many of the industrial enterprises depended on relatively skilled workers and these craftsmen found it relatively easy to create unions organized around their craft skills. When larger-scale industry did develop, the craft unions were able to provide an experienced cadre of personnel to assist in organizing the new industrial unions. Industrial unions face a more sophisticated task of organization since they have to combine different occupational and skill categories into a cohesive unit. In developing countries, however, the work force is less well prepared to undertake these organizational tasks. There are few experienced leaders within the country. There usually is no indigenous craft-union tradition on which to draw. Many of the highly skilled and experienced workers are likely to be drawn from outside the country and, thus, are culturally different from the other workers. Therefore the stability that can come from effective union organization is unlikely to develop.

Too, most developing countries have had colonial backgrounds and much of the economic development in these countries have had colonial origins. Within these countries, the independence movement often used working-class unrest as the integral element. Thus, nationalist movements often subsume working-class movements. After independence, dissatisfaction of the work force within the modern sector is often assumed to derive from the inability to reduce the colonial and dependent status of the society. Particularly if the employers are foreign, either because of colonial memories or because of governmentally invited economic development, such discontent is often seen as being a consequence of the continued exploitation.

Middle-class nationalists, including intellectuals, have usually considered the attempt to organize workers to be an integral part of strengthening the nation. They also have recognized that workers, when organized, offer concentrated political power that can be used in other ways. Workers, frustrated by their limited power, often respond to the more inclusive appeals of nationalism and liberation as being a quicker and more certain route to their own economic improvement. The nationalist issues that do become involved in labor disputes, however, often obscure the economic and job-security issues that relate more directly to the employees. Thus, middle-class nationalist leadership often sharpens labor protest but, on the other hand, it is often not successful negotiating with individual employers. In such a context, working-class protest may tend to become politically disruptive rather than economically effective.

To new governments in developing societies, disruptions from working-class protest seem extremely threatening. Whereas the same behavior prior to independence was considered to be highly desirable, when it occurs in a postindependence context the government is likely to see it as disloyalty. But these governments may also recognize that the existing trade unions are too ineffective to establish collective bargaining relationships with their employers. Lacking an effective voluntary industrial relations system, the state often has to intervene in such disputes. Such intervention usually is oriented toward helping the worker develop the work-welfare conditions that have been developed over time in other industrial societies. The state often assumes the responsibility for assuring these conditions by establishing governmental programs or other forms of governmental encouragements. The long-run effect of such state intervention is to inhibit the growth and development of viable trade unions since the state can provide a much more powerful and effective force to implement workers' desires. Such intervention is not always altruistic. Governments usually have as an objective creating in the minds of the worker a sense of loyalty to the state and, more narrowly, toward the particular party in power. In democratic systems, the party in power, seeking to remain there, makes use of various techniques to tie the unions and the labor movement to it. Such a potent political base as labor usually guarantees the party's retention of power.

The party in power often has another reason for becoming involved in labor disputes, sometimes contradictory to their political dependence on labor. A new state, almost invariably, is committed to a program of economic development. Sharp and extended conflict between workers and employers can be disruptive to such development. By being in the middle, however, the state is caught in an agonizing dilemma—what may be politically expedient for the worker may be catastrophic for the course of economic development. But only governments who stay in power can face this dilemma.

Much of what has been said about the development of industrial relations in developing countries fits Curaçao and was basic to the labor difficulties that led to the disturbance. In Curaçao's pattern of industrial development, the domination of one industry tended to preclude the development of a strong craft-union tradition. Skilled workers were brought to the island who were different culturally and often racially from the unskilled workers and therefore did not provide learning and organizational skills to create a viable union structure. Consequently, the union picture is fragmented and diffuse. Among the dock workers and construction workers, several unions competed for the allegiance of the workers, and often loyalty to a union was achieved by the actions of charismatic leadership, often only tangentially concerned with economic issues.

The continuity of Shell and its associated companies from the colonial period and its economic dominance on the island provided a basis for charges of continued colonialism. (Although the pattern of damage on May 30 suggests that Shell has come a long way in overcoming this image and now tends to be seen as an insider.) The attempt by the government to attract foreign investment and the economic concessions that were necessary added support to a claim of continued colonialism. Of course, throughout the dispute, union leaders used nationalist symbols in an attempt to gain support for their economic claims. When nationalist movements lack their own symbols, they often borrow symbols that convey the success of nationalist and liberation movements elsewhere. For example, in Curaçao certain labor leaders affected revolutionary khaki uniforms and were rather dramatic figures riding around the island in their jeeps, symbols that could hardly be missed.

The labor disputes placed the government in a dilemma that could not be easily resolved. The Democratic Party could not afford to lose its critical labor support but, on the other hand, neither could it let its efforts to attract new industrial development, which many saw as a longer-run solution to economic problems, be threatened by excessive wage demands. Nor could the government risk long and disruptive labor disputes.

The focus of the march on May 30 — Fort Amsterdam — indicated where the unions felt the locus of economic power and final decision-making was located. Prior to the march, union leaders wondered aloud why the government did not "tell" WESCAR to settle the strike. What was initially an economic issue became transformed into a political issue, and the fact that the government was forced to resign indicated not only the political potential of the unions but also the close relationship that was seen by many of the workers between economic and political injustice.

Following the emergence of the May Movement and the success of the Liberation Front at the polls, there was an increase in union membership and greater union solidarity. On the other hand, the coalition of union and nationalist interests within the Liberation Front proved rather unstable. The more pragmatic political and economic goals of the union leaders conflicted with the more abstract and idealistic goals of the nationalist themes, represented by Stanley Brown. Over time, the union solidarity that had developed began to show cracks along the same divisions that had separated them previously.

THE MAY MOVEMENT AND RACIAL
DISTURBANCES IN THE UNITED STATES

The emergence of the May Movement in 1969 was frequently seen as being somehow related to the much more publicized black rebellions that had erupted in such American cities as Los Angeles, Newark, Detroit, and Cleveland during the 1960s. There were certain similarities, as well as differences, between them. The May Movement and the black rebellions in the United States were alike in that they were attacks upon traditional societal arrangements that worked to the disadvantage of nonwhites and the economically depressed. They were collective efforts by such groups in the two societies to create more satisfying social arrangements. The movements in the two countries were also similar in that as they developed they became increasingly political in character. As in Curaçao, the initial demands of participants in the black protest movements in the United States were often vague, coming as they did during periods of proto-political violence. But, like their counterparts in Curaçao, protest leaders in the United States helped transform the uprisings into political protest by more clearly specifying demands and by calling for such changes as greater political representation for blacks, more and better jobs, and in some cases even demanding the resignation of mayors, police officials, and other authorities.[6] And also as in Curaçao, protest leaders in the United States attempted to give the urban movements more organization by coordinating attempts at pressuring white officials into acting favorably on such demands. Given such similarities, were the consequences of the May Movement similar to those generated by the movements in the United States?

The May Movement did follow the pattern of the recent protest movements in the United States in having consequences for the protesting, disadvantaged group as well as for the larger society.[7] The protest in the two societies ushered in periods of innovation and experimentation within the disadvantaged communities. A willingness to try new solutions to old problems resulted in the emergence of many new groups and organizations. For example, after the May Movement emerged in Curaçao the Liberation Front and MAN were established along with new unions. Similarly, within the black community in the United States, new economic, cultural, and political groups calling for self-determination for the black community were born following the urban uprisings. In Los Angeles, the militant cultural organization US was formed, as well as SLANT, a group with black-power ideology. In Detroit, a militant organization known as the Citywide Citizen's Action Committee was created for the purpose of achieving black control of the black community. In Chicago, black police officers organized the Afro-American Patrolmen's League to protect the interest of the black community in police affairs. The urban uprisings in the United States also played a role in the emergence of militant black unions and black student organizations. Why did these new groups and organizations emerge within the nonwhite, disadvantaged communities in both Curaçao and the United States? They emerged because the protesting groups believed that existing groups and organizations were incapable of solving their problems. In both Curaçao and the United States, then, some of the most important changes were generated within the communities from which the protest came.

Societies cannot ignore major protest movements but must react to them in some fashion. Given the threat they posed to traditional social arrangements, the May Movement and the black protest movements in the United States forced established groups and authorities into making certain adjustments. And in broad terms the adjustments made by established groups and authorities in the two countries were similar. That is, on the one hand, efforts were made to make certain changes and reforms in response to some of the grievances articulated by the movements and, on the other hand, actions were taken to counteract and limit the power of the movements. From the standpoint of the movements themselves, such consequences represented gains and losses.

We have already described the successes of the May Movement in detail. The political gains included the success of the Liberation Front at the polls during elections for both the central and island governments, the increased political influence of labor, the fall of the old government and the greater flexibility of the new, and the selection of blacks for such high public office as prime minister and governor of Curaçao. On the economic and social front, unions negotiated an unusual number of wage hikes, the business community became less insensitive to labor, some social restrictions against nonwhites were lifted, and change-oriented organizations like the Curaçao Development Corporation and Obra y Logra were formed.

Reforms are usually made grudgingly in societies and Curaçao was no exception. Established groups give up power and privilege only to the extent that they feel it is necessary to do so. Thus as reported earlier, so far as the protestors were concerned, a number of unintended changes also occurred in Curaçao because of the May Movement. Some of the changes that were made by established groups and authorities were designed to counteract and limit the power of the May Movement or to shore up their own lagging power. For example, The National Party and URA reunited in an effort to recoup losses suffered at the hands of the Liberation Front at the polls. Former prime minister Kroon organized MASA in an attempt to recapture some of the influence he had enjoyed in Curaçao politics prior to the May Movement. Also, the government took steps to strengthen the capacity of the police and voluntary corps to control future rebellions.

In the United States, too, from the standpoint of the protestors, both desirable and undesirable changes resulted from the protest movements of the 1960s. On the plus side, political, business, and civic leaders in the United States became more responsive to black grievances. Thus some local political authorities saw the need to hire more black police officers, to organize community relations groups, and to establish ghetto city-hall offices ostensibly to give ghetto residents easier access to local government and reduce their sense of isolation. Also, urban task forces were formed to tackle some of the myriad political, economic, and social problems that plague black Americans.[8] In some cities, leading white businessmen, educators, and government officials joined with black leaders to form problem-solving groups like the New Detroit Committee and the Committee of Concern in Newark.[9] Public and private organizations also endeavored to improve employment and educational opportunities for blacks. And efforts were made to improve housing for blacks and to expand recreational programs in some communities.[10] The federal government enlarged or initiated new programs in several communities following the uprisings. The Office of Economic Opportunity was a major supporter of these programs. Many new black groups and organizations received much of their financial backing from federal agencies and private sources such as corporations and foundations who because of the urban protest movements felt the need for some change and reform in the society.

Yet, as in Curaçao, there were also actions taken in the United States to counteract and resist the potential power of the black protest movements. For example, white segregationist groups emerged in the wake of the protest.[11] Also, steps were taken by authorities to increase the capacity of law enforcement agencies to control future rebellions. Riot plans were written, riot training for law enforcement personnel was greatly expanded, and new riot-control equipment was purchased. There is evidence which suggests that the major response to the rebellions in many cities in the United States involved such control measures.[12]

These, then, were some of the similarities in the changes generated by the May Movement in Curaçao and the black protest movements in the United States. We can now raise the question: How successful was the May Movement in achieving change in Curaçao compared to the recent protest movements in the United States? This question cannot be answered with a high degree of precision. It is not clear, for example, whether the May Movement was more or less successful than the protest movements in the United States in making progress toward solving some of the economic problems of the poor. Even with the prodding from the movements in Curaçao and the United States, programs established in the two countries for this purpose were meager and inadequate given the size of the task. It seems somewhat safer to say, however, that the May Movement had greater immediate political effect than the protest movements in the United States.

The political changes generated in Curaçao by the May Movement by no means altered the basic position of the masses. Yet the changes appear to be somewhat more significant than those generated by the recent protest movements in the United States. This seems so even if we only consider the fact that the government was forced to resign in Curaçao whereas this was never a real possibility in the United States. However, other things also point to the conclusion that the May Movement might have had a greater political impact than the protest movements in the United States. As noted, the May Movement produced two genuine political parties, the Liberation Front and MAN, that won legislative seats. Also labor acquired more political influence in Curaçao as a result of the May Movement. They were consulted more often by the government and a new labor department was created in recognition of their new status and the increased significance of labor matters. Furthermore, blacks were appointed to high government offices following the emergence of the May Movement. It does not seem that the protest movements in the United States had this type of immediate political impact.

A number of factors can explain the different political significance of the protest movements in the two societies. First, even though the rebellions in the United States tended to move from proto-political violence to political action as the May Movement in Curaçao had done, the latter assumed a more organized political form. This may have been partly due to the involvement of key existing groups, the labor unions, at the very beginning of the protest in Curaçao that at the right moment could serve as the core for more organized political behavior. This moment came when, in the wake of the May 30 violence and destruction in Willemstad, the unions formed a coalition and called for the resignation of the government. In the United States, comparable existing groups apparently did not get as thoroughly involved in the protest actions as the labor unions in Curaçao. The success of the labor coalition led to even more organized political activity, that is, the formation of a new labor party. This turn toward party politics by some of the May Movement dissidents, which also ultimately resulted in the formation of MAN, was furthered by the ease in which political parties can be formed in Curaçao and offer candidates for office, and a political history that has seen the birth of many small parties.

Structural factors also seem to have been involved in the dissimilar political consequences the protest movements had in the two societies. A large and highly developed society like the United States has a greater capacity for controlling dissidence and thus avoiding change and reform than a small, developing society like Curaçao. Not only does the United States have the technical resources for minimizing disruption over the long run, but the organizational resources as well. Thus, whereas the Antillean government had to rely on outside assistance in quelling the violence in Willemstad, the United States, with its well-trained police, armed forces, and National Guard units, handled the internal threats to its stability with relative ease. It was more difficult, then, for government officials in Curaçao than those in the United States to avoid making some political concessions to groups who threatened to call for renewed violence unless reforms were made. The different social-control capacities of the two societies is underscored by the fact that sometime after the May 30 violence in Curaçao the United States supplied the Curaçao police force with riot equipment.

The size of the aggrieved groups in the two societies also undoubtedly had some bearing on the different political consequences of the movements. In the United States, blacks comprise approximately 11 percent of the population whereas in Curaçao the vast majority of the inhabitants are nonwhite. Thus again it was more difficult for authorities in Curaçao than those in the United States to ignore the demands for change and reform since they were coming from those who were part of the majority group in the society.

The different historical experiences of the United States and Curaçao might also have been related to their varying political responses to collective protest. In contrast to Curaçao, the United States has had a long history of riots, rebellions, and protest movements.[13] In addition to race riots, the United States has experienced antidraft riots and movements, abolition movements, slave rebellions, and a stormy history of labor-management relations. This history would seem to mitigate to some extent the impact of the black protest movements of the 1960s. Curaçao, on the other hand, has not had a history of civilian protest and rebellion. Relations between the races had been considered good when compared with other multiracial societies. Furthermore, given the paternalistic nature of employers and the fact that the labor movement is relatively new, there has not been a history of labor turmoil on the island. Consequently, when the May Movement exploded on the scene, its impact was enhanced by the fact that no one expected it and it was the first movement of its kind to emerge in Curaçao. Thus the greater immediate political gains of the May Movement might have in part resulted from the fact that it was viewed as a more serious threat than the rebellions in the United States.

The May Movement achieved certain black power goals, such as the appointment of a black prime minister and governor, that would have made black power movements in the United States and elsewhere somewhat envious. Yet the May Movement was not truly a black power movement. To be sure, MAN had a black platform and the Liberation Front called for an end to the oppression of blacks. It is also true that many high government and police authorities blamed the May 30 violence on "black power elements in Curaçao." Nevertheless, black power or black nationalism was not the basic thrust of the May Movement. As we have already suggested, a more significant dimension of the movement was Antillean nationalism. This was evident in the movement's call for equal wages for Antilleans, more and better jobs for Antilleans, and recognition of the Antillean language, Papiamento. This is not to deny, of course, that the racial issue was a very important part of the protest. Clearly it was, and it is not difficult to understand why given the fact that the under class in Curaçao was overwhelmingly nonwhite. Still, however, the black power theme never became the overriding one during the May Movement as was true of the protest movements in the United States during the 1960s, and the revolt in Trinidad in 1970.[14] This might have been because the Netherlands Antilles has not had a history of black nationalist thought and activity.

In contrast to Curaçao, in the United States, where black nationalism has had a long tradition, the black protest movements were one of the major factors that helped foster a revival or resurgence of nationalist sentiment and programs in the black community during the 1960s. Groups spawned by the protest—for example, SLANT, US, and the Afro-American Patrolmen's League—emphasized black nationalism, or black power, and would undoubtedly have applauded even the modest political success achieved by the May Movement that we have mentioned.

One final note might be made in our comparison of the political consequences of the May Movement in Curaçao and the recent protest movements in the United States. In both countries, government-appointed commissions were charged with investigating the violent phases of the movements. Such commissions were told to seek the causes of the violence and to recommend measures that might prevent their recurrence.

A riot commission was established by the Antillean government in October, 1969. Five Antillean and three Dutch members were appointed to it, the latter upon the recommendation of the Dutch government. The eight-member commission included four sociologists, an engineer, a lawyer, a retired judge, and a government employee with a doctorate in theology. The commission gathered data on the May 30 violence and its causes through confidential interviews with citizens of Curaçao. All segments of the island were invited to present their views. Some public hearings were also held by the commission. The commission completed a report on its investigations at the end of May, 1970.

How successful was the Antillean riot commission? If its success is judged in terms of its effectiveness in getting the government to act on its recommendations, then perhaps it was no more successful than such commissions in the United States as the National Advisory Commission on Civil Disorders, more commonly known as the Kerner Commission. Lipsky and Olson, for example, minimize the significance of the Kerner Commission as well as other commissions because they have generally failed to convince government authorities to implement their major recommendations.[15] As in the case of the Kerner Report, the report of the Antillean commission was met with official silence by the government.[16] Some changes were eventually implemented in Curaçao that had been suggested by the commission in its report. For example, the government appointed a new lieutenant governor with considerable police experience to head the police force in Curaçao. The commission had been highly critical of the actions of the police during the violence on May 30, and suggested the need for such a change. Also, as had been recommended by the commission, the government began making fewer appointments based on patronage. However, it is difficult to tell if these changes were made because of the commission's report, although at least one of the commissioners expressed the view that he thought so. But even if such changes were made as a result of the efforts of the commission, the vast majority of the commission's recommendations were not implemented. However, a different conclusion might be reached regarding the success of the Antillean commission if it is judged on a slightly different basis. For example, Campbell suggests that the true test of the significance of commissions lies in whether or not they present important facts about national problems to those in positions of power and to the public.[17] Based on this perspective, then, the Antillean commission, as Campbell suggests was also true of the Kerner Commission, did meet with some success. The Antillean commission wrote a hard-hitting report in which problems of the society were spelled out, especially those relating to politics. In contrast to what many critics felt the Kerner Report failed to do, the report by the Antillean commission clearly spelled out what were thought to be the government's contributions to the underlying and immediate causes of the May 30 violence. This included statements about political patronage and favoritism, governmental isolation from the masses, especially labor, and police incompetence. A number of factors could possibly have contributed to such forthrightness. First, the composition of the commission might have been important in this regard. As noted, there were Dutch as well as Antillean members on the commission. Thus even if the Antillean members had come under pressure from local authorities to tone down the criticism of the Antillean government, it might have been difficult to do so given the presence of the Dutch who would have been less affected by such pressure. Perhaps even more significant was the fact that the administration that was in power at the time of the violence was no longer in office and thus could not exert pressure on the commission to deliver a report that cast it in a favorable light. Finally, the commission was prodded by radical factions like Vitó to objectively portray the shortcomings of government in the Netherlands Antilles. It is interesting to note that the man who had been initially appointed as head of the commission resigned before its work was completed. Prior to his resignation, he had come under heavy fire from Vitó.

## THE MAY MOVEMENT AND OTHER WESTERN SOCIAL MOVEMENTS

Although we have put the events in Curaçao in the context of the May Movement, it is also necessary to place the movement in a much more global context. Although all social movements are oriented toward change, Turner has suggested that social movements that have the greatest impact in the long run are those which are able to create a new sense of what is *just* and what is *unjust* in a society.[18] While the focus of attention of a particular social movement may be a problem of long standing within a society, what is changed is that what was once considered a misfortune comes to be viewed as an injustice. The difference between a sense of misfortune and a sense of injustice among a significant part of the population is seen in the difference between petition and demand. Those who have been the victims of a misfortune can petition those in power to help them, but the victims of an injustice will demand that their petition be granted. As Turner has suggested:

> A significant social movement becomes possible when there is a revision in the manner in which a substantial group of people look at some misfortune, seeing it no longer as a misfortune warranting charitable consideration but as an injustice which is intolerable in society. A movement becomes possible when a group of people cease to petition the good will of others for relief of their misery and demand as their right that others ensure the correction of their condition.[19]

If one looks at the history of Western Europe, there have been times in which the concerns in various societies have been dominated by a particular sense of injustice. Two major eras can be delineated. In the liberal humanitarian era, exemplified by the American and French revolutions, people demanded the right to participate in ruling themselves. There was the insistence that people should no longer merely petition their rulers but that society should be structured in such a way that all people can be heard and participate in governing themselves. This was the new right. It was at the time a radical idea, particularly for those in power. Socialist movements later retained the symbolism of freedom and participation but insisted on the right of people to demand the essential material needs of life. This was also a new idea. Even to many of the early liberal humanitarians, preoccupied with political rights, poverty was still considered a misfortune, not an injustice. This was changed when various movements, ranging from the more radical communist and socialist movements in Western Europe to the New Deal in the United States, pushed for the idea that a society was obliged to provide for material wants.

Turner has suggested that, in the West, a new revision is now in progress with a new object of indignation. Today, for the first time in history, the idea is being put forth that people have a *right* to personal worth. It is an old theme, biblical and otherwise, that a person is to be pitied who does not feel worthy and cannot find his identity. But to consider this as an injustice is new and to suggest that society needs to guarantee a sense of personal worth for every person must be considered radical. Identity may have been seen as desirable in the past but it has hardly been considered a right. In many contemporary social movements, however, the key complaint is phrased in terms of alienation. This theme is particularly strong among the young, involved in student movements, in rather affluent societies. In such societies, the political right to participate is now assumed; economic right for material support is now assumed; but still man has not been provided a sense of personal worth. Now this too must be guaranteed. In this context—the process of transforming misfortunes into injustices—many of the elements present in Curaçao can be placed.

In Western Europe and in the United States, the various periods with their dominant concerns have extended over several hundred years and have, of course, been "solved" in various ways—the first, by various forms of political democracies and the second, by variations of the welfare state. Now, in most of these societies, particularly among the young, the predominant focus of injustice merging is centered upon problems of identity. Whereas most

Western societies ''solved'' these problems in a somewhat sequential manner, in Curaçao, all of the eras, and particularly the first two, have been telescoped in time. The island's close ties to Western Europe and to the United States did provide a continuous channel for various ideas concerning injustice. Liberal humanitarian ideas, of course, have been present on the island for a long time, as evidenced in the abolition of slavery, but one could argue that the final acceptance of a new norm of political participation did not become institutionalized in effect, until the change in colonial status making Curaçao a semiautonomous part of the Kingdom of the Netherlands in 1954. There has been somewhat concurrently a focus on the theme of economic injustice relating to unionization, bargaining rights, and minimum wages. This discussion has been sharpened in recent years with increasing concern with unemployment created by automation in the refineries and with increasing economic expectations, at least in part prompted by the impact of mass media and by the influx of tourists with a vacationer's attitude toward spending money. A sense of economic injustice was the initiating focus of the May Movement.

Also present in Curaçao were elements of the third era. Students returning from being educated in the Netherlands brought back knowledge about the various political and countercultural movements that are current in Western Europe. There was contact and interest in various movements within the Caribbean, such as Castroism and various black power ideologies. In turn, black power ideologies within the Caribbean are strongly influenced by what is happening in the United States. There are also influences that come from Latin America, particularly from Catholic radical sources. Although the impact of these influences is perhaps overestimated by many on the island, they tend to become blended into a more general theme of Antillean nationalism, expressed rather dramatically in the Vitó movement. But elements of all three themes of injustice—political, economic, and identity—came together and combined in a particularly explosive way on May 30 and continued in the context of the May Movement. By contrast, most of the Western societies have been able to deal with each of these three dimensions of injustice more sequentially.

## THE CONSEQUENCES OF THE MAY MOVEMENT
## FOR THE CURAÇAO OF THE FUTURE

While we have concentrated on the short-term changes that resulted from the May Movement, it is useful in this concluding statement to project its impact much further into the future. Hoetink, in his discussion of types of race relations in the Caribbean, uses the concept *segmented society* to describe a particular type of society.[20] By a segmented society, he refers to one that, at its point of origin, consists of at least two groups of people of different races and culture, each having their own social institutions and social structure. While each of the segments has its own rank within the social structure, such a society as a whole is governed by one segment. The historical Curaçao is described by this concept. Hoetink contends that in such segmented societies, there are only two theoretical possibilities for further structural development—they can remain segmented or they become more homogeneous.

Remaining segmented, however, necessitates agreement on the justice of the segmentation. Historically, such justification has usually derived from a religious belief structure that provides an orderly hierarchical world such as that which supported the caste system in India or from an amalgam of religious and racial ideology that characterized the deep South in the United States and, more recently, South Africa. Segmentation constitutes the conditions in which there are no marginal groups within the society since each is in its proper place. The problem of finding clear examples of contemporary segmented societies suggests the difficulties in maintaining segmentation.

Among the factors undercutting the justification of segmentation have been the social movements in the West that have emphasized political and economic injustice. As ideological justifications are undercut, it produces the conditions that facilitate the process of homogenization. Homogenization can proceed either by the elimination of one segment by one or more of the other segments or by the gradual racial and cultural mingling of the original segments. The elimination possibility has never been considered as a realistic alternative in Curaçao. On the other hand, the gradual mingling, partly racial but mostly cultural, has gone on from the very beginning.

Hoetink suggests that a segmented society initially goes through a stage of "pseudo-homogenization" in which the dominant segment attempts to maintain the society in terms of its own image. At the same time, since there is no ideological justification to support the segmented arrangement, the other groups within the society do not accept it and become marginal to the dominant cultural tradition. Such widespread marginality becomes an important force for change in the direction of further homogenization within the society.

In the early history of Curaçao, the Dutch Protestants attempted to keep themselves and Curaçao in tune with the Netherlands, reproducing the architecture, feverently identifying with the king, and stressing everything that was Dutch. The presence of the Sephardic Jews on the islands created problems for the view of Curaçao as a simple extension of the Netherlands. For a long time, they were treated as a separate nation—"the Portuguese nation"—and separated from the Dutch by language, residential locations on the island and, of course, by religion. Over time, the significant part the Jews played in the economy of the island made it difficult to consider them as somehow separate. Too, liberal tendencies in the treatment of religious groups in the Netherlands affected Curaçao since it was the model to follow. As various actions became normative in the Netherlands, Jews also began to be accepted into governmental positions in Curaçao and the role that they already played economically was recognized. In turn, for the gradual recognition, the Jews increasingly emphasized their Dutchness, for example, by accepting the language in their synagogue activity. Both the increasing, even if begrudging, acceptance of Jews into the society and the modifications that occurred within the Jewish community to reduce their differences were a part of the on-going process of homogenization.

The presence of the blacks on the island presented a different set of problems for the pseudohomogenized view of the Dutch Protestants. The role of Curaçao in the slave trade was created by the interests of the Dutch West India Company. Slavery, in itself, could fit into a pseudohomogenized view of Curaçao. By treating people as property, it was not necessary to treat them as being members of the society. Slavery allowed the basic Dutchness to remain without major contradiction. Only those who were white were members of the society; those who were not were neither "real" nor permanent members. But the ideas of human dignity and freedom coming into the island were also "Dutch." The decline of the slave trade and its economic consequences also resulted from religious and political considerations present in Europe. These considerations led to pressure to reduce and eliminate the trade. As slavery was ending, some other way of treating the blacks was necessary. One temporary adaptation was at least to keep Protestantism white and Dutch when Curaçao could not be. Hartog reports that in 1816 when the slave trade was ending and the emancipation of all slaves was being anticipated, there were only a few white Catholics; and all free colored, except twenty, and all slaves belonged to the Roman Catholic Church.[21] Such an arrangement allowed the white Protestants to maintain the fiction of being an extension of the mother country while keeping the blacks in a separate religious category. Such adaptations were temporary since other factors continued to undermine the Dutch Protestant pseudohomogenization. The decline of the economic fortunes of Curaçao during the nineteenth century resulted in out-migrations by some of the Dutch and by some Jews. On the other hand, with fewer economic opportunities and with larger families, the black Catholic population almost doubled.

The intensity of Dutch Protestants' desire to maintain their image of the society was also reflected in the discussion about voting rights cited in Chapter two. Since property qualifications would shift the balance of political power to the Jews and a more general franchise would shift it to the blacks, there was contentment to leave the political destinies of Curaçao in the good hands of the colonial office. In fact, a broadened franchise for voting was finally ''forced'' on Curaçao. There is no doubt, however, that over time it was becoming increasingly difficult to continue to maintain the posture of homogeneity around Dutch Protestant values.

The ultimate break in the historical illusion came about when the Dutch began to see themselves not just as a numerical minority but increasingly as a cultural minority. Ironically, what facilitated this feeling of minority consciousness among the Curaçao Dutch was the building of the refinery. Those Dutchmen coming to the island with the technological skills necessary for the construction tended to see the locals as rather quaint, isolated colonials. It must have been traumatic for the locals to have spent so much energy to maintain their Dutchness and then to find that they were not only unappreciated but even rejected by the modern European carriers of the ''authentic'' culture. So it was now clear to the whites that though Curaçao was a variant of Dutch culture, it had a distinctive Caribbean stamp. This recognition and self-discovery led to the emergence of island nationalism. There was increasing emphasis on Papiamento, which symbolized the separation that was being recognized and the uniqueness that was being affirmed. Distinctions such as *makamba* and *landskind* became more than linguistic descriptions. These same themes were later an integral part of the May Movement.

This feeling of estrangement from the Netherlands and the growing feeling of unity among the groups on Curaçao led to pressure toward independence. The motives among the various segments within Curaçao were different—most in Curaçao had never belonged so independence was a recognition of what had always been true. For the Dutch Protestants it would symbolize what had somehow happened. The independence movement itself tended to foster feelings of solidarity among the various segments on the island. With the severance of the colonial ties and with the new found local autonomy, many of the formal barriers that would prevent Curaçao from deciding its own destiny were dissolved. The homogenization, which was the inevitable outcome of living and working together for hundreds of years, had already come a long way but it was far from complete. Although much unity had been achieved, the political party system as it evolved after independence tended to reflect and perpetuate in certain ways the older segmentation. With the help of the labor movement, the Democratic Party that symbolized the white Protestant interests was able to continue its dominance.

The May Movement was, then, a further step in the continuing homogenization among the various segments within Curaçao. The distinction that emerged during the violence between the insider and the outsider was not a matter of color or class but primarily a distinction of where one's loyalties were placed. Since the question of political loyalties had been solved by the earlier break with the Netherlands and the internal autonomous status, the pivotal question in the May Movement was one of economic loyalties. Those merchants and employers who were outsiders were the targets. The political consequences that the May Movement had were somewhat unanticipated but they resulted in the greater involvement by groups, particularly blacks, that had been traditionally excluded. The May Movement was one further step, a traumatic one for many, in the inexorable process of Curaçao moving toward its own identity.

One of the more striking features in Curaçao today is still the presence of what can be called multiple minority consciousness. Each group within the society tends to think and feel in minority terms: black, colored, or white; Catholic, Protestant, or Jew; old or new resident; upper middle or lower class; young or old. The social locations that had provided the secure anchors of identity for the Dutch Protestants have crumbled. Although slavery tore the roots of the blacks, a return to Africa, even emotionally, makes no sense, nor do the various black movements in the Caribbean or in the United States. They may create local interest but seldom provide direction. Although many of the residents of Curaçao are black, they are Curaçao blacks. The Jews of Curaçao have had the advantage of hundreds of years of marginality. And, in fact, it was our observation that the Jews on Curaçao were able to see the May Movement as less of a personal threat than were the Dutch Protestants. Many Jews played rather key roles in the immediate reconciliation process. Among the groups on the island, the major similarity was their common Antillean identity—this, they shared, regardless of other differences.

This common identity, however, already was important and, in spite of our emphasis here on the violent aspects, there were important indicators that interpersonal relationships on the island were in many ways very strong. There is the startling fact that, even with the enormity of property damage on May 30, the level of personal violence was very low. Two persons were killed and most of the injuries were of the kind that required first aid rather than hospitalizaton (just for contrast, in racial disturbances in the United States, 26 were killed in Newark, 34 in Watts, and 43 in Detroit). It is also important to note, that though a large number of vehicles were burned, no drivers were injured. This includes the car that was stopped by marchers in which the driver was defined as symbolizing racial injustice. Such drivers were harassed somewhat by the crowd, and they were obviously indignant, but the separation of person and property was carefully made. In addition, it is likely that, during the disturbance, if shop-owners had not closed their shops and gone home, fewer shops would have been looted. Shop-owners who stayed were generally not bothered.

What this suggests is that the prior reputation of Curaçao of having relatively good relations among the various groups did have a basis in fact and that it was reflected in mitigating the nature and extent of personal violence. The attack was primarily in terms of definition of property and its use by outsiders. The interpersonal ties transcended the potential divisiveness of race and class and provided a degree of cohesiveness that prevented an even greater explosiveness.

The primary message of the May Movement was an outgrowth of the historic segmentation of Curaçao in which the blackness, low status, and the lack of political power were combined within the segmented working class. This class, however, had had a major role in Curaçao's past and wanted to have a continuing part in the direction of the future. Their investment, they felt, was being threatened. Late on Friday, May 30, an older white resident was leaving Willemstad and as he stood at a vantage point looking back at the smoke and flames throughout the city, he said to a young black passing by, "Look at *your* city." The young black replied, "That's not *my* city." This brief conversation symbolized both the tragedy of that day as well as its ultimate meaning for the future of Curaçao. The young black was not aware that his reluctance to claim the city was widely shared in groups that historically had been dominant. No segment could now be sure that Curaçao was "his." In his angry reaction, however, the young black missed the implication that it was now *his* city. The May Movement emerged in this ambivalence—the desire to belong and the doubt as to whether one did belong. No single segment could be sure that the city (the society) was "his." Even so, the May Movement did become a major step in bringing closer the diverse groups in Curaçao, which had been brought together by the accidents of history. Underneath the conflict, the May Movement highlighted the element that all groups in Curaçao had in common—their Antillean identity. With this bond strengthened, the debate on the future of Curaçao could go on.

---

1. Adrain H. Jones and Andrew R. Molnar, "Combating Subversively Manipulated Civil Disturbances," The American University, Center for Research in Social Systems (Washington, D.C., October, 1966), p. 14.

2. For a more detailed elaboration of the view reported here see, E. L. Quarantelli and Russell R. Dynes, "Property Norms and Looting: Their Patterns in Community Crises," *Phylon* 31, no. 2 (Summer, 1970): 168–82.

3. For observations on the selectivity of looting, see Russell R. Dynes and E. L. Quarantelli, "Organization as Victim in Mass Civil Disturbances," *Issues in Criminology* 5, no. 2 (Summer, 1970): 181–93.

4. Alvin and Helen Gouldner, *Modern Sociology* (New York: Harcourt, Brace and World, 1963), p. 218. A more comprehensive statement is that "property is the name for a concept that refers to the rights and obligations and privileges and restrictions that govern the behavior of man in any society toward the scarce objects of value in that society." This

158    Social Movements, Violence and Change

definition and a general discussion of property is presented in David Sills, ed. *International Encyclopedia of the Social Sciences*, 12:590.

5. See Morris D. Morris, "Labor Relations: Developing Countries," *International Encyclopedia of Social Sciences*, 8:510–16.

6. Unless otherwise indicated, our observations regarding the recent black protest movements in the United States are taken from William A. Anderson, "The Reorganization of Protest: Civil Disturbances and Social Change in the Black Community," *American Behavioral Scientist* 16, no. 3 (January–February, 1973).

7. Several of our informants indicated that there were at least three distinct communities in Curaçao: a business elite, a government elite, and a predominantly nonwhite community consisting of laborers and the poor and intellectuals who identify with them.

8. Urban America, Inc. and the Urban Coalition, *One Year Later* (New York: Praeger, 1969), chap. 7.

9. National Advisory Commission on Civil Disorders, *Report of the National Advisory Commission on Civil Disorders* (New York: Bantam Books, 1968), pp. 152–53.

10. Ibid., pp. 154–56.

11. Ibid., p. 153.

12. Ibid., p. 151.

13. See, for example, Hugh Davis Graham and Ted Robert Gurr, *Violence in America: Historical and Comparative Perspectives* (Washington, D.C.: U.S. Government Printing Office, June, 1969).

14. For a discussion of the 1970 black power revolt in Trinidad see, Ivar Oxaal, *Race and Revolutionary Consciousness* (Cambridge, Mass.: Schenkman, 1971).

15. Michael Lipsky and David Olson, "Riot Commission Politics," *Trans-Action*, July/August, 1969.

16. "30 Mai, 1969: Rapport van de Commissie tot onderzoek van de archtergroden en oorzaken van de onlusten welke op 30 mai 1969 op Curaçao hebben plaatsgehad" (Willemstad, mai 1970).

17. James S. Campbell, "The Usefulness of Commission Studies of Collective Violence," in *Collective Violence*, ed. James F. Short, Jr., and Marvin E. Wolfgang (Chicago: Aldine Atherton, 1972).

18. Ralph H. Turner, "The Theme of Contemporary Social Movements," *British Journal of Sociology* 20, no. 4 (December, 1969). For a description of the transformation of the labor movement, see Gaston V. Rimlinger, "The Legitimation of Protest: A Comparative Study in Labor History," *Comparative Studies in Society and History* 2 (April, 1960).

19. Turner, "The Theme of Contemporary Social Movements," p. 391.

20. H. Hoetink, *The Two Variants in Caribbean Race Relations: A Contribution to the Sociology of Segmented Societies*, pp. 109–19.

21. J. Hartog, *Curaçao: From Colonial Dependence to Autonomy* (Aruba, N.A.: De Wit, Inc., 1968), p. 286.

# APPENDIX A

# The Agreement of Kralendijk*

The following parties:

—Democratic Party of Curaçao;

—Partido Patriótico Arubano;

—Frente Obrero y Liberación 30 di Mei;
(Labor and Liberation Front May 30)

—Democratic Party of the Windward Islands;

—Partido Obrero Boneriano jointly with Partido
Progresista Boneriano Uni;
(Bonairean Labor Party jointly with United Progressive Bonairean
Party):

declare in principle that after extensive deliberations and negotiations
they have reached an agreement on the basis of which it was decided to
cooperate with each other towards the formation of a Government for the
Netherlands Antilles.

This agreement takes as its point of departure the standpoint that this
statement of principles is definitive, but it will furthermore be based on a
statement of principles and basic points of a Government Policy Pro-
gramme. The latter will be worked out in detail by the participating

*Akwerdo Di Kralendijk, Netherlands Antilles Government Pamphlet (November,
1969).

factions in common consultation, and each faction will hand to the Cabinet informer a written contribution as soon as possible.

They declare, moreover, that no extension of the number of Ministerial seats is aimed at, while in accordance with the existing seats the following distribution is advocated:

FOR THE DEMOCRATIC PARTY:

Economic Affairs

The policy of this Department shall be changed thusly that in principle solely native born citizens can get an establishment permit for businesses in the retail trade. Also, the flight of capital shall be combated.

With due observance of the insular autonomy, the federal government shall promote tourism—both within and outside the Netherlands Antilles—inter alia by coordinating this economic pillar.

Economic Development

The policy of this Department shall be aimed also at promotion of local industry, tradesmanship and home industry.

For the purpose of attracting industry from abroad, through agencies of the federal government and of the Kingdom, the federal government shall take care of a reasonable spreading of such industries over the various island territories of the Netherlands Antilles.

Finance

The income tax must be further socialized, and this must find expression in the progressivity of the levy.

The credit-giving policies of the Popular Credit Bank and the Building Credit Bank must be revised, to make these institutions better adapted to the purpose they were founded for.

Education

The policy of this Department shall be aimed at producing within the shortest time an orthography of the Papiamento language and, when this has been achieved, to introduce this language on the Leeward Islands, one and the other as a basis for the eventual adoption of Papiamento as the communications vehicle.

Culture and Education

Promotion of physical development for the population of the Netherlands Antilles, by the practice of sports. The policy shall also be set at retaining and promoting an own Antillean culture.

FOR THE PARTIDO PATRIÓTICO ARUBANO

General Affairs

Parties agree that this Cabinet post is attached to the function of Minister President.

Justice

The policy of the Justice Department shall be aimed at achieving, within the shortest span of time possible, a complete modernization and adaptation of the police and prosecution apparatus. Articles 136a and others of the Criminal Code, dealing with matters concerning public order, shall be deleted.

Communications

The policy regarding the communications media of radio and television must be such, that these in their utilization shall express the freedom of speech and free manifestation of opinion, this in keeping with the freedom of the Press.

FOR FRENTE OBRERO Y LIBERACIÓN 30 DI MEI

Social Affairs
Labor

These two departments shall within the briefest period of time possible achieve the following urgent provisions:

(a)   introduction of a regulation setting a minimum wage for all laborers;

(b)   enactment of a federal ordinance setting up a compulsory pension fund for enterprises and private institutions, alongside the existing General Old Age Insurance;

(c)   introduction of a General Sickness Act for the entire population of the Netherlands Antilles;

(d)   introduction of an Act regulating dismissals (layoffs);

(e)    enactment of the legal obligation governing the recognition by employers of labor unions and of lawful representatives of employers' and employees' organizations;

(f)    formation of a committee consisting of representatives of labor unions, with the task of advising the Government on labor matters;

(g)    introduction of a general unemployment insurance comprising all workers;

(h)    revision and adaptation of labor legislation.

The Government in its entirety, shall take steps to see to it that the workers employed by all Curaçao Mining Company Ltd. will not lose their livelihood as the consequence of the complications with that Company.

Public Health

The policy of this Department shall be aimed at liberalizing the law regulating the admission of physicians in such sense, that more physicians and pharmacists who graduated from foreign recognized universities, can be admitted here.

The federal ordinance on pharmacy is to be adapted to modern philosophies.

Parties declare that—in proportion to the number of their seats on the legislative Council of the Netherlands Antilles—they shall have a voice in and be represented in all Government agencies and commissions, the 'Antillean Home' (i.e., the office of the Minister Plenipotentiary in The Hague) and representations abroad.

Moreover, when appointing the Governor, the Acting Governor, Lt. Governors of the Island Territories and Administrators, the wishes of the cooperating parties shall be taken into account on the same basis.

The manifested needs of the island territories of Bonaire and the Windward Islands, shall merit the especial attention of the entire Council of Ministers.

The distribution of seats on the Council of Ministers shall be as follows:

for the Democratic Party                                          3 seats

for the Partido Patriótico Arubano                               3 seats

for the Frente Obrero y Liberación 30 di Mei                     2 seats

The replacement of Ministers shall be arranged within the same party, except the function of Minister-President.

Furthermore it has been decided that the following functions or posts shall be filled as detailed below:

| | |
|---|---|
| Chairmanship of the Legislative Council | Democratic Party of Curaçao |
| Vice-chairmanship of the Legislative Council | Partido Patriótico Arubano |
| Vice-premiership | Democratic Party |
| Minister-Plenipotentiary in The Hague | Democratic Party. |

In principle it is also agreed upon, that all problems and identification of problems of a nature of principle, shall be the subjects of discussions both between the Ministers of the cooperating factions as well as between their respective factions, in order to achieve a joint formulation of decisions.

Efforts will be made towards acquiring the greatest possible measure of social security for all strata of the population of the Netherlands Antilles.

The general objectives will have to comprise:

maintenance of order, peace and safety, with full respect for the rights of man, revision of our political position in the Kingdom, creating the opportunity for the Antilles to determine their own standpoint with relation to international problems;

reforming of the structure of the insular system of government, especially in the financial and political fields, achieving a liberalization of the insular autonomy;

increase of social activity;

increase of production and productivity of labor, both in the material and the non-material sphere, and through this enhancing the national income.

It must be set as a central point of attention, that a just distribution of the national income is necessary, by devoting especial care to creation of job opportunities for those able to work.

The Informer is empowered by the above-mentioned Parties to bring contents of this Declaration of Principles to the attention of the Governor.

The Informer is, moreover, authorized to notify the Governor of the fact, that the purpose of the instructions of the Governor to the Informer dated September 22, 1969, has been complied with, to wit: that the new Government can bank on a two-thirds majority of the Legislative Council, in order to secure the social, economic and political future of the Netherlands Antilles.

Also, they place on record in conclusion that their joint efforts will always be aimed at the general interest of the Netherlands Antilles.

This Statement of Principles will be issued in the form of a pamphlet in Papiamento, English and the Netherlands language, and distributed amongst the population of the Netherlands Antilles.

Thus agreed upon in Kralendijk, Bonaire, on November 23, 1969, and signed by the representatives of:

DEMOCRATIC PARTY OF CURAÇAO

S. G. M. Rozendal
H. L. Braam
P. A. van der Veen
O. R. A. Beaujon
C. D. Kroon
F. J. Pijpers
R. M. Martinez
A. A. Jockheer
S. W. Rigaud
C. E. Cathalina

DEMOCRATIC PARTY OF THE WINDWARD ISLANDS

A. C. Wathey

PARTIDO PATRIÓTICO ARUBANO

O. Croes
L. A. I. Chance
E. R. Finck
R. O. Pretonia
G. A. Oduber

PARTIDO OBRERO BONERIANO JOINTLY WITH PARTIDO PROGRESISTA
BONERIANO UNÍ

- J. M. Frans
- E. R. Domacasse
- D. J. Egbrechts
- A. F. Sealy
- R. E. Martijn
- F. G. Janga

FRENTE OBRERO Y LIBERACÍON 30 DI MEI

- W. Godett
- A. P. Nita
- S. C. Brown
- N. G. Monte
- H. M. Thomas
- C. G. Hurtado
- J. Smeulders
- R. A. Pketersz

KABINETSINFORMATEUR—E. O. Pretonia

# APPENDIX B

Conclusions and Recommendations, *May 30, 1969:*

*Report of the Commission for the Investigation*

*Of the Causes of the May 30, 1969,*

*Riots on Curaçao*

CONCLUSIONS

1. From the investigation it is concluded that, although on the evening of May 29 different groups were planning to hold a demonstration, there are no clear indications of a premeditated, organized mass march to town.

2. The Commission could not find any indication of a premeditated organized conspiracy for mass arson, looting or plans to overthrow the Antillean Government, nor indications of the oft-heard opinion that the occurrences on May 30 were instigated by foreign interference or by the Black Power organization.

3. For the most part, the arsonists were not selective in the buildings they destroyed.

4. The Commission is of the opinion that, in spite of the racial problems which are clearly evident in the Caribbean area, the racial element did not play a predominant role on May 30th.

5. The WESCAR conflict cannot be considered as an isolated occurrence but should be seen as a climax of several labor conflicts in the six months preceding May 30th.

6. The incompetent way in which this labor conflict was approached by all the parties involved—employer, employee and the Government—led to an escalation of tension and conflict which would help explain the explosive outbreak on May 30th.

7. The WESCAR conflict only can be seen as the direct cause of the occurrences on May 30th. The basic causes should be sought in:

a) the existing differences in wage scale between the oil industry and the other sectors of the economy;

b) the large structural unemployment, which had been generated in the last ten years;

c) the recent growing gap in standard of living differences within the community, of which the people had become more conscious through a greater awareness of the economic circumstances and relative differences in Western Europe and North America;

d) the more and more inadequate arrangements experienced in the field of social welfare;

e) the widening gap between the Government on the one side and the people, particularly the trade union movement, on the other side;

f) the primacy of economic development (over social welfare), a primacy reinforced by the influence of economic assistance;

g) favoritism in official matters of persons and companies on grounds of purely political considerations, which favoritism, rightly or wrongly, is accepted by an important part of the population as an established fact.

8. The existent feeling of dissatisfaction was considerably intensified and radicalized by increasing criticism of a group of young intellectuals and quasi-intellectuals.

9. The Commission is of the opinion that the police force failed in the execution of its duty to maintain order on May 29 and 30 because of a failure of leadership, planning, communication and coordination. The numerical strength and armament of the police force of Curaçao probably would have been adequate to control the disturbances on the evening of May 29 and during the morning of May 30 if the force had been led by capable leaders with the right tactical approach.

Finally, the Commission is of the opinion that the premature conviction of the police authorities that the police force was not able to control the difficulties by itself and that military assistance was necessary were of direct influence on the lack of energetic and effective command.

10. The above mentioned points indicate factors which made the request for military assistance during the morning of May 30 inevitable.

11. While the Commission on the one hand was impressed by the skill and leadership of some Antillean union leaders, on the other hand, it cannot be denied that militant irrational elements in the union movement strengthened their grip on the striking laborers so that the bona fide union leaders lost, to a considerable extent, their influence on them.

12. The Commission, finally, is of the opinion that only the interaction and convergence of the above mentioned factors could have led to the disturbances of May 30th.

SELECTED RECOMMENDATIONS

1. The Central Government must always keep close control of the police force to be sure that its management is in capable hands.

2. The police force is in urgent need of a good alarm system in case of serious public disturbances. This should be accomplished as soon as possible.

3. Now more than ever the police chief should increase the confidence of the force in its own strength in order to prevent the call on military assistance in the future.

4. The Commission is of the opinion that the introduction of compulsory education should be done in a short period of time.

5. The Commission is of the opinion that the introduction of Papiamento in the basic grades on the Leeward Islands will facilitate the change from family to school environment.

6. The Commission wishes to point out that attention should be given to the introduction of special education programs for children of less fortunate social and cultural backgrounds.

7. The influence of party political considerations when appointing civilian personnel is disapproved by the Commission. Due to the shortage of manpower which the Netherlands Antilles struggles with for the time being, only a policy of "the right man in the right place" can guarantee a responsible execution of the task which rests upon the Government.

8. The Government should reorganize its financial aid (support and loans of the Volkskrediet bank) so that in reality as well as appearance political favortitism is prevented.

9. Appointment of nonpolitical persons to the Government Information Service would improve the communication between the Government and the people.

10. Regarding the structural unemployment problem, the Government and private sector should take all possible steps to attract foreign investors to the Netherlands Antilles. In addition local initiatives in trade and industry should be promoted.

11. The Commission considers it inevitable that in the future a general minimum wage law will be introduced. Before the introduction of such a law, a thorough study of its implications should be made.

12. For development policy, a balanced division between economic and social projects is recommended. The Dutch Government should, when reformulating its program of financial aid to the Netherlands Antilles, support such a policy.

13. More than ever trade and industry should give more attention to education within their firms through which the upward flow of lower personnel could be accelerated as places become available.

14. Much more attention will have to be paid to personnel-management and guidance, as well as to industrial relations.

15. The Commission thinks it advantageous that the Curaçao trade unions develop stronger bonds among themselves and work towards a unified organization.

16. It is necessary to think about the possibility of creating compulsory unemployment insurance.

17. The Commission also suggests the introduction of:
    —relief support, according to the minimum demands of the cost of living;
    —child support, considering the desirability of birth limitation;
    —large grant support to private institutions for social work.

18. An adequate representation of the Negro population in the highest government offices without allowing this to result in any form of reverse discrimination.

# APPENDIX C

# Data Collection

Data for this study were collected on field trips to Curaçao in 1969, 1970, and 1971. Field work was begun by the authors three weeks after the May 30, 1969, violence had erupted. A week was initially spent in Curaçao gathering information on the violence and on the sociohistorical background of the Netherlands Antilles. On this first trip we also established contact with persons whom we thought would be valuable sources of information on later field trips that we had planned. The second data gathering field trip was made to Curaçao in June, 1970, just after the first anniversary of the May Movement. Nearly a month was spent doing field work in Curaçao on this trip. A third field trip was made to Curaçao in July, 1971, more than two years following the outbreak of the 1969 violence. On this final trip we completed the field work in two weeks.

The initial focus of the study was on the May 30 violence. We had initially decided to study the role of various groups and organizations in Curaçao during the violence, both those groups and organizations that had actively participated in the violence and those which had played a role in trying to control it. However, our preliminary research indicated quite clearly that the May 30 violence was but one part of a larger social movement and that it could be understood sociologically only to the extent that this was taken into account in our analysis. Thus the focus of the study was expanded to include other aspects of the May Movement in addition to its violent phase. Part of this expansion included research on the impact of the May Movement during a two-year period rather than just on its immediate consequences.

The principal sectors of Curaçao involved in the drama surrounding the May Movement were governmental and political groups, business organizations, and those groups which comprised or supported the labor movement. Thus the better part of the field work on this study was concentrated on these groups and organizations. The primary source of data was semistructured interviews with key informants from the above-mentioned groups and other groups and organizations in Curaçao. The interviews were aimed at eliciting information on the underlying conditions that led to the May Movement, the dynamics of the movement, and the changes it generated in Curaçao. These interviews were conducted in English and they averaged about an hour and a half each. These formal interviews were generally done at a group's headquarters or office. However, some were also conducted in different settings; for example, a few interviews were conducted in a sidewalk cafe in one of downtown Willemstad's main public squares, and one was even done in the hospital room of a labor leader who had been shot during the May 30 violence. In addition to the formal interviews, many informal interviews were also conducted. These took place during social occasions, such as during dinner when we were able to secure supplementary information pertaining to the study through conversation with knowledgeable persons. Frequently informal interviews were later followed up with more formal ones or provided leads to important new contacts.

We received excellent cooperation from those we approached for interviews. Our initial contact in Curaçao was a businessman who was also noted for his years of voluntary service on the island. He simplified the task of entreé by providing us with introductions to many of the key groups and organizations in Curaçao. However, we wanted to become gradually independent of him so that we would not become overly identified with one segment of Curaçao.[1] This was accomplished as the persons we interviewed introduced us to others that we wanted to see, thus enabling us to rely less and less upon the assistance of our initial contact. With a few exceptions, those we interviewed provided us with very straightforward answers to our questions. We tried to allay any fears that respondents might have had in answering frankly by assuring them that they would remain anonymous. In most cases, this was sufficient to gain their cooperation. There were no outright refusals to be interviewed and in several cases we interviewed persons more than once. It is not clear whether or not the fact that we were an interracial team, one black and the other white, contributed to the excellent cooperation we received from all segments of Curaçao. A total of 62 interviews were conducted. The interviews were from the following groups and institutional sectors of Curaçao.

*Government*

Office of the Prime Minister; Office of the Governor-General; Office of the Lt. Governor of Curaçao; Curaçao Department of Economic Development; Department of Social Affairs

*Political Parties and Movements*

May 30 Labor and Liberation Front; Vitó; Union Reformista Antillano; Democratic Party of Curaçao; National People's Party; MAN

*Labor*

CCV; AHU; AVVC; CFW; PWFC; BTG; NAVA; ABVO

*Economic*

WESCAR; Shell; Maduro and Sons Inc.; The Veps Group Inc.; Curaçao Chamber of Commerce; CODECO

*Special*

Riot Commission

*Military*

Royal Dutch Marines; Curaçao Voluntary Corps

*Civil Service*

Curaçao Police; Curaçao Hospital; Ministry of Health; Curaçao Public Works; Curaçao Port Authority

*Voluntary Service*

Red Cross; First Aid; Obra y Logra; Joint Service Club Committee

In addition to the interviews, written materials were also collected for this study. Newspapers published on the island were used as a supplementary source of information. Also many groups and organizations made available to us records and reports that were relevant to our study. The riot commission, for example, provided us with copies of its report.

---

1. Murch, for example, comments on the importance of this in his study on the French Antilles: "Generally, one should avoid becoming identified with any one contact or group of contacts, particularly if the researcher seeks the cooperation of competing political, economic, and social groups." Arvin Murch, *Black Frenchmen: The Political Integration of the French Antilles* (Cambridge, Mass.: Schenkman Publishing Co., 1971), p. 144.

# INDEX